ENJOY RETIREMENT

A SIMPLE GUIDE TO DISCOVERING FUN, SATISFACTION, AND NEW ADVENTURES IN YOUR GOLDEN YEARS

NEAL M. KENWICK

© **Copyright Neal M. Kenwick/ Michawell LLC, 2024. All rights reserved.**

The content within this book may not be reproduced, duplicated or transmitted without direct written permission from the author or the publisher.

Under no circumstances will any blame or legal responsibility be held against the publisher, or author, for any damages, reparation, or monetary loss due to the information contained within this book. Either directly or indirectly. You are responsible for your own choices, actions, and results.

Legal Notice:

This book is copyright protected. This book is only for personal use. You cannot amend, distribute, sell, use, quote or paraphrase any part, of the content within this book, without the consent of the author or publisher.

Disclaimer Notice:

Please note the information contained within this document is for educational and entertainment purposes only. All effort has been expended to present accurate, up-to-date, and reliable, complete information. No warranties of any kind are declared or implied. Readers acknowledge that the author is not engaging in the rendering of legal, financial, medical or professional advice. The content within this book has been derived from various sources. Please consult a licensed professional before attempting any techniques outlined in this book.

By reading this document, the reader agrees that under no circumstances is the author responsible for any losses, direct or indirect, which are incurred as a result of the use of the information contained within this document, including, but not limited to, — errors, omissions, or inaccuracies.

CONTENTS

Introduction   5

1. Embracing Technology for Leisure and Connection   7
2. Budget-Friendly Fun   23
3. Physical Health and Wellness   39
4. Mental Engagement and Lifelong Learning   55
5. Social Connections and Community Building   71
6. Travel and Adventure   85
7. Emotional Health and Personal Growth   103
8. Creative and Cultural Pursuits   119

Conclusion   133
References   137
Author Biography   141

INTRODUCTION

Retirement isn't a final chapter; it's a door swinging wide open to a garden of transformative possibilities. It's a time when fun, growth, and adventure bloom with vibrant intensity. This isn't just hopeful thinking—it's a reality that eagerly awaits each person who steps into this phase of life, ready to explore it with enthusiasm.

With this book, my aim is not just to redefine what it means to retire, but to guide you through this transition. I present retirement not as the sunset of one's life, but as a vibrant new dawn ripe with potential. My vision is to lead you through the discovery of a range of activities that are tailored to fit a variety of interests and physical capabilities.

This book is crafted to not only inform but also to inspire and motivate you, offering pathways to maintain your health, expand your social circles, and continue personal growth. Structured around themes such as embracing technology, finding budget-friendly entertainment, nurturing your health and wellness, engaging your mind, fostering social connections, exploring new destinations, managing emotional health, and pursuing creative outlets, this book addresses the broad spectrum of interests that you may have or wish to explore.

As we turn the pages together, remember that retirement is your time to thrive. It's a period for self-discovery, adventure, and deepening the enjoyment of life. I invite you to approach your retirement years with curiosity and optimism, ready to fill each day with the new and the wonderful.

Let's embark on this journey together, reshaping the narrative of retirement into one of excitement and ongoing satisfaction. Welcome to your golden years—an era not just to be lived but celebrated.

CHAPTER 1
EMBRACING TECHNOLOGY FOR LEISURE AND CONNECTION

When my mother-in-law first retired, she felt like she was missing out on the daily connections that had filled her bustling career life. However, her perspective changed dramatically when her children introduced her to the marvels of a smartphone. Within weeks, she was not only in constant touch with her loved ones but had also discovered a host of apps (applications) that made her day-to-day life more manageable and enjoyable.

This transformation is not unique to her; it represents a powerful shift that technology can bring into your life, especially as you age. Technology has revolutionized how we connect, learn, and enjoy leisure time. For seniors, mastering this technology can open a world of opportunities, enhance daily life, and maintain meaningful connections with friends and family.

1.1 Mastering Smartphones: A Beginner's Guide to Apps and Features

Understanding Smartphone Basics

For those who might feel daunted by the array of buttons, icons, and apps on a smartphone, let's break down its fundamental features. A smartphone is essentially a phone meant not only for making calls and sending texts but also for accessing the internet, using various applications, and much more. The first step is understanding the home screen, the first screen you see when unlocking your phone. Here, you'll find icons representing different apps, each serving different functions. Making calls is straightforward with the phone app, usually symbolized by a green icon with a phone handle. Text messaging, on the other hand, is handled through the messages app, typically indicated by an icon resembling an envelope or speech bubble. Adjusting settings like sound, brightness, and connectivity is done through the settings app, often represented by a gear icon. Familiarizing yourself with these icons and their functions is the first step in harnessing the power of your smartphone.

Introduction to Essential Apps

Beyond the basic features, smartphones can be enriched with numerous applications that cater to various needs. Essential apps that can enhance your daily life include weather apps, which provide daily and weekly weather forecasts; news apps that keep you updated on local and global events; and health-tracking apps, which monitor aspects of your health and remind you of medication schedules. Installing these apps involves accessing a digital store on your phone—Google Play for Android users and the App Store for iPhone users. You can search for the needed app here and press 'install' to add it to your device. Once installed, these apps appear on your home screen or within the app library, ready for use.

Enhancing Communication

The ability to stay connected with family and friends is one of the most significant benefits of modern smartphones. Messaging apps like WhatsApp allow you to send messages, photos, and videos and even make voice and video calls over the internet, often for free. Video call platforms like Skype or Zoom can help you join family gatherings, celebrate milestones, or simply chat face-to-face with loved ones across the globe. These apps require a one-time setup, typically requiring you to create an account with an email address. Once set up, you can add contacts by entering their phone numbers or connecting to them through the app's search function. Engaging with these apps can significantly enhance your connection with family and friends, making distances feel shorter.

Customizing the Smartphone Experience

To make your smartphone truly yours, you can personalize it in several ways. Adjusting the font size to make text easier to read can be done via the settings menu under the 'display' option. Changing your wallpaper to a favorite photo or a pleasing design can add a personal touch to your phone. Furthermore, smartphones allow you to organize your apps by grouping them into folders, keeping your home screen tidy and your favorite apps easy to access. This customization not only makes your smartphone more enjoyable to use but also ensures it meets your specific needs and preferences.

Incorporating these elements into your smartphone use demystifies the technology and turns it into a tool for keeping your life organized and staying connected with your social circles.

1.2 Silver Surfers: Navigating Social Media to Stay Connected

Social media platforms have become vibrant hubs of activity where people of all ages gather to share news, photos, and ideas and maintain connections with family and friends. As a retiree, engaging in these digital communities can significantly enrich your social life and connect you to the broader world. Each platform has its unique flavor and purpose, which can cater to different interests. Facebook, for instance, is excellent for staying in touch with family and friends, sharing updates, and joining groups of like-minded individuals, whether they revolve around gardening, books, or travel. Instagram appeals to those who prefer visual storytelling through photos and videos, ideal for sharing experiences like meals, travels, or daily activities. On the other hand, Pinterest serves well for those interested in gathering ideas on everything from recipes to craft projects, allowing users to create and manage inspiration boards.

Setting up social media accounts is your first step towards joining these vibrant communities. Begin by visiting the website or downloading the app of the platform you choose. You will need to provide basic information such as your name, email address, and password to create your account. Navigating the privacy settings immediately after creating your account is crucial. These settings control who can see your posts and your profile details and who can send you friend requests or messages. Take time to understand these options, typically found in the settings menu, and adjust them to suit your comfort level when sharing personal information.

Engaging with content on social media is straightforward and rewarding. To post updates on Facebook or Instagram, you can use the status or photo upload features. These platforms allow you to share text updates, photos, or videos, which you can enhance with captions. Commenting on posts by friends or within groups can also be a delightful way to interact and share your thoughts. Joining groups is particularly beneficial as it connects you with people who share similar interests. On Facebook, for instance, you can find groups for nearly any hobby or interest area, which can be an excellent source of information and camaraderie. Participating in these groups not only helps you stay informed about topics you care about but also builds a supportive network of friends who can turn into your virtual community.

When it comes to safety and privacy on social media, a cautious approach is advisable. Be mindful of the personal information you share, such as your home address, phone number, or any financial information. It's wise to limit this sharing to private messages with trusted individuals rather than in public posts or comments. Additionally, be skeptical of requests from people you do not recognize and be wary of clicking on links that seem suspicious or out of character from your known contacts, as these could be attempts to compromise your privacy or security. Social media platforms frequently update their security features, so keeping informed about these can help you maintain a secure online presence.

Navigating social media can be a fulfilling adventure, allowing you to maintain existing relationships and cultivate new ones, all from the comfort of your home. With these tools at your fingertips, you can continue to grow your network and enjoy social interactions, which are crucial for a happy and fulfilling retirement.

1.3 Online Learning: Platforms for Enhancing Knowledge and Skills

The digital age brings unprecedented access to knowledge and learning that transcends traditional classroom boundaries. For those in retirement, online learning platforms like Coursera, Khan Academy, and Udemy offer a treasure trove of opportunities to not only brush up on old skills but also dive into new subjects. Imagine delving into the mysteries of ancient history, mastering the basics of digital photography, or even understanding the intricacies of computer programming—all from the comfort of your home. These platforms cater to a wide array of interests and provide courses designed by top-notch universities and industry leaders, ensuring high-quality learning experiences that are both engaging and educational.

Registering on these platforms is a straightforward process. Start by visiting the website of the platform you choose, where you will find an option to sign up, usually at the top right corner of the homepage. You'll need to provide some basic information, such as your name, email address, and password. After registration, navigating these sites is quite intuitive. Each platform has a search function that allows you to find courses by entering keywords related to your interests. Once you find a course that intrigues you, further information can be accessed by clicking on the course title, which will take you to a detailed page with descriptions, instructor bios, course content, and user reviews. These insights can help you make an informed decision about whether to enroll. Enrolling is usually as simple as clicking an 'Enroll' button, and many courses offer the flexibility to start immediately or on a set date.

The advantages of engaging in lifelong learning are substantial, particularly for seniors. Studies have shown that continuing to learn new skills can lead to improvements in memory and overall mental health. But beyond these cognitive benefits, there is also a profound emotional gain. Learning new things can provide a sense of accomplishment and purpose, which is especially significant during retirement years when many might feel like they are losing their sense of identity previously tied to their professional life. Furthermore, the joy of discovery that comes with learning can be a significant mood booster and help fight feelings of loneliness.

Engaging with online communities associated with these learning platforms can further enhance the educational experience. Most platforms include forums where learners can exchange ideas, ask questions, and provide support to one another. Participating in these communities can deepen your understanding of the subject matter and connect you with people from all over the world who share your interests. This interaction can foster a sense of global community and belonging, which is invaluable. For instance, after completing a photography course, join a group where members critique each other's work, provide constructive feedback and encouragement, or share opportunities for photography outings or online exhibitions.

The landscape of online learning is vast, offering endless possibilities for exploration and growth. Whether you dive deep into a subject you've always been passionate about or explore entirely new territories, the wealth of knowledge available at your fingertips is a powerful tool for personal development and enjoyment. Through these platforms, learning can continue to be a vibrant part of your life, enriching your days with new understandings and connections. As you navigate these sites and engage with their content, you may find that learning is not just an activity but a profound source of joy and fulfillment, bringing new energy and enthusiasm to your retirement years.

1.4 Virtual Travel and Tours: Exploring the World from Your Living Room

The advent of technology has not only transformed how we connect and learn but also how we experience the world around us. Virtual travel and tours offer a unique opportunity to traverse the globe from the comfort of your living room, bringing the wonders of the world right to your fingertips. This exciting digital realm allows you to visit museums, national parks, and iconic landmarks without the need to pack a suitcase or even step outside your front door. Platforms like Google Arts & Culture and Virtualtrips serve as gateways to these experiences, offering a range of tours that cater to diverse interests. Google Arts & Culture, for instance, partners with thousands of institutions to provide access to famous works of art, historical artifacts, and cultural treasures from around the globe. Virtual trips, on the other hand, hosts live tours with guides who interact with viewers in real-time, providing a dynamic and engaging virtual experience.

When exploring virtual tours, you might start with a visit to the Louvre in Paris to marvel at the Mona Lisa, then switch to a live walkthrough of Yellowstone National Park, all while discussing the sights with fellow virtual tourists from around the world. These platforms are designed with user-friendliness, ensuring that navigating through them is straightforward. Typically, you would visit their website and browse through the available tours. Each listing details the tour, including the duration, the critical sights covered, and any interactive features available. Selecting a tour is as simple as clicking on it and following the instructions to join live or view a pre-recorded session. This flexibility allows you to tailor your virtual travel experiences to match your schedule and interests, making it an ideal way to explore new destinations or revisit cherished places.

Beyond the joy of discovery, these virtual tours serve a practical purpose in planning future travels. As you immerse yourself in these experiences, keeping a journal or a digital document where you can note down places that capture your heart is helpful. Whether it's the vibrant streets of Barcelona or the serene landscapes of the Japanese countryside, each virtual visit can help you gather ideas for your travel itinerary. These notes can include specific sites you want to explore further, local foods you'd like to taste, or cultural events you wish to attend. This preparatory step enhances your anticipation and ensures that when the time comes to turn these virtual experiences into real adventures, you are well-prepared with a personalized and meaningful travel plan.

Utilizing streaming services like YouTube can further enrich your virtual travel experiences. Various channels specialize in travel documentaries and guided tours, providing detailed insights into the destinations' historical contexts, cultural significance, and natural beauty. Watching these documentaries can deepen your understanding of the places you visit virtually, adding layers of knowledge and appreciation that enhance the overall experience. For instance, before virtually visiting the Taj Mahal, watching a documentary about its history and the architectural marvels of Mughal, India can make your virtual tour more engaging and informative.

Interactive elements like 360-degree photos and maps offer another dynamic layer to virtual travel. Platforms incorporating these technologies allow you to view destinations from various angles and perspectives, giving you a more comprehensive sense of the place. For example, interactive maps can be used to virtually walk through a neighborhood in Rome, exploring side streets and local cafes, while 360-degree photos can transport you to the summit of Mount Everest, offering panoramic views that are breathtakingly close to reality. Engaging with these features brings a sense of adventure. It helps you appreciate the complexities and beauty of different landscapes and cultures worldwide.

Whether you're looking to understand the world better or simply seeking inspiration for your next trip, these digital adventures promise enriching experiences that can be enjoyed alone or shared with friends and family. As you continue to partake in the vast offerings of virtual travel, remember that each tour is more than just a visual experience; it's a stepping stone to more excellent adventures in the vibrant, ever-expanding world beyond your screen.

1.5 Utilizing Technology for Health Management and Fitness Tracking

In the realm of health and wellness, technology has carved a path that allows us to monitor and manage our health with remarkable ease and precision. Consider the evolution of health apps like MyFitnessPal and Fitbit. These tools empower you to take charge of your physical activity, dietary habits, and even medication schedules with just a few taps on your smartphone. Such apps have transformed how we approach our health, offering tailored insights and real-time data that help us make informed lifestyle decisions.

Health apps like MyFitnessPal allow you to track your dietary intake by logging meals and snacks. This can be incredibly helpful in managing weight or maintaining a balanced diet, especially for those managing conditions like diabetes or heart disease. The app breaks down the nutritional content of your food, providing detailed information about calories, fats, carbohydrates, and proteins. This level of detail makes it easier to understand your dietary habits and make necessary adjustments to improve your health. Similarly, fitness trackers like Fitbit not only count your steps but also monitor your heart rate, sleep patterns, and overall activity level throughout the day. They can even remind you to move if you've been inactive for too long, a fantastic feature for maintaining mobility and enhancing physical health.

Wearable technology has seamlessly integrated into our daily lives, offering an unobtrusive method to keep our health checks in line. Devices like Fitbit or the Apple Watch sync wirelessly with smartphones, providing notifications and summaries of your daily progress. They can monitor your heart rate continuously, crucial for detecting heart conditions early or monitoring recovery posthospitalization. Some of these devices are also equipped with fall detection, alerting emergency services and family members if a fall is detected, providing peace of mind for you and your loved ones. The simplicity with which these devices integrate into daily life and their user-friendly interfaces make them an excellent choice for seniors keen on maintaining their independence and monitoring their health.

Telemedicine has also emerged as a pivotal component of modern healthcare, particularly valuable when visiting a doctor in person is not feasible. This technology allows you to speak with healthcare providers via video conferencing, making medical advice more accessible than ever. Platforms like Teladoc or Doctor on Demand provide services where you can talk to a provider, renew prescriptions, and even receive a diagnosis through your computer or smartphone. To use these services, you should set up an account, provide some medical history, and then schedule an appointment that can be conducted from anywhere you have internet access. This consulting method is incredibly beneficial for routine checkups or non-emergency medical issues, as it saves time and reduces the stress of commuting.

Staying informed about health is another area where technology can play a significant role. Reliable sources such as the Mayo Clinic or WebMD offer a wealth of information that can be accessed easily online. These resources keep you updated on the latest health guidelines, treatments, and research in an easy-to-understand language. They often feature tools like symptom checkers or medication dictionaries, helping you understand potential health issues and treatment options. However, while these resources are valuable, it's always best to consult with a healthcare provider for a diagnosis or before making any significant changes to your treatment plans based on information you find online.

Embracing these technological tools can significantly enhance your ability to manage your health independently, allowing you to enjoy your golden years with confidence and vitality. Whether tracking your nutrition, monitoring your physical activity, consulting with doctors online, or staying informed about health topics, technology offers multiple avenues to ensure that you are at the helm of your health journey.

1.6 E-Commerce Simplified: Shopping Online Safely and Efficiently

The digital landscape offers a plethora of shopping opportunities that bring convenience to your doorstep. Platforms like Amazon and eBay have revolutionized the way we shop, providing access to a vast array of products from the comfort of our homes. Setting up accounts on these platforms is the first step toward unlocking a world where anything from groceries to gardening tools is just a click away. To begin, you'll need to visit the website of your chosen platform and look for the 'Sign Up' or 'Create Account' button, usually located at the top of the page. The process involves entering some basic information such as your name, email address, and a secure password. Once your account is set up, navigating these sites is straightforward. The home page typically displays a search bar at the top, where you can type keywords for the items you're interested in. Each item's page provides detailed descriptions, pricing, and shipping options, making it easy to understand your purchase.

Ensuring that your online transactions are secure is crucial. Start by checking that the website address begins with 'HTTPS' rather than just 'HTTP.' The extra 'S' stands for 'secure' and means that all communications between your browser and the website are encrypted. This is especially important when entering sensitive information such as credit card details. Speaking of credit cards, using them for online purchases is often safer than using debit cards because they offer better fraud protection. Most credit card companies react quickly in case of suspicious activity and don't hold you liable for fraudulent charges. Additionally, consider using payment services like PayPal, which provide an extra layer of security as you don't need to input your credit card information directly into the website.

Comparing prices and reading reviews are next in ensuring an informed purchase. Most online shopping platforms feature comparison tools that allow you to see prices from different sellers simultaneously, helping you find the best deal. Additionally, customer reviews can be invaluable. They not only provide real-world feedback on the product but also on the seller, offering insights into their reliability and service quality. Take your time to read through these reviews, as they can help you avoid products that may not meet your expectations despite appearing suitable online. Look for patterns in reviews; a single negative review could be an outlier, but several similar complaints might indicate a consistent issue with the product or seller.

Finally, understanding the return process is an essential aspect of online shopping. Most platforms have a section detailing their return policies, usually found at the bottom of the website. These policies outline how long you may return an item, what condition it must be in, and whether you'll pay for return shipping or receive a refund or exchange. If you decide to return an item, you'll typically need to print a return label from the website. This label should be attached to the package before dropping it off at a shipping provider or scheduling a pickup. Being familiar with the return process can alleviate much of the stress associated with online shopping, as you know you can return items that don't meet your expectations.

Navigating the world of online shopping can initially seem daunting. Still, once you become familiar with these platforms, you'll find they offer a convenient and efficient way to make purchases. Whether you're buying everyday necessities or indulging in a hobby-related purchase, the digital marketplace provides all the tools you need to make safe, informed, and satisfying transactions. Remember, the key to a positive online shopping experience lies in taking proactive steps to ensure your transactions are secure, comparing prices, reading reviews, and understanding the return policies. With these practices in place, you can enjoy the convenience and variety of online shopping without undue stress.

Overall, using these digital tools and resources can enhance your ability to stay connected, informed, and engaged in various aspects of life.

CHAPTER 2
BUDGET-FRIENDLY FUN

R etirement unfolds a new canvas, inviting you to paint your days with vibrant experiences that don't stretch your wallet. Embracing this newfound freedom doesn't mean you have to spend extravagantly. The world around you combines enriching, cost-effective, and delightful activities. From the quiet halls of museums to the bustling energy of community festivals, this chapter will guide you through various local attractions and events that promise enjoyment without a hefty price tag.

2.1 Exploring Local Attractions: Museums, Parks, and Historical Sites

Utilizing Local Free Days

Many cultural institutions like museums, zoos, and botanical gardens offer free entry days to the public, making it an ideal opportunity to explore these venues without a financial burden. These free days are typically listed on the institutions' websites under a 'visitors' or 'tickets' section. Additionally, local newspapers and tourism websites often have calendars listing upcoming free days. Subscribing to newsletters from these cultural institutions can also inform you about free entry opportunities, special events, or temporary exhibitions. This way, you can strategically plan your visits, ensuring you make the most of these offerings. These experiences enrich your understanding of art, history, and science and provide an excellent backdrop for social outings with friends who share your interests.

Discovering Parks and Outdoor Spaces

Local and state parks are treasures that await your exploration, often requiring little to no fees. Whether you're into hiking, bird watching, or simply enjoying a picnic under the sky, these natural reserves offer a plethora of activities. Most parks have well-maintained trails; many provide detailed maps at entrance points or on official websites. These maps often highlight points of interest, such as scenic overlooks, historical sites, or areas where wildlife is frequently observed. Engaging with nature benefits your physical and mental health, providing a serene environment to unwind and reconnect with the natural world. Grabbing a field guide from your local library can enhance this experience, turning a simple walk into an educational endeavor where every leaf and bird song adds to your understanding of the ecosystem.

Participating in Community Events

Your local community is a vibrant hub of activities, many of which are free or cost very little. City websites, community bulletin boards, and local libraries typically have event calendars that detail upcoming events such as parades, art shows, craft fairs, and festivals. These events offer entertainment and a chance to meet new people and engage with your community. Participating or volunteering at these events can enrich your experience, making you an active participant in the tapestry of your local culture. Festivals often celebrate specific aspects of local culture, history, or seasonal harvests, providing a deeper appreciation and connection to your community.

Exploring Historical Sites and Landmarks

Many towns and cities are rich with history, hosting landmarks and sites that tell the story of the area's past. Exploring these historical treasures can be a fascinating outing, often available through self-guided walking tours. These tours provide exercise and educate you about the historical significance of the buildings, monuments, and sites in your locality. Local historical societies often offer maps and brochures for these tours, which can be picked up from local tourism offices or downloaded from their websites. As you walk these routes, you'll gain insights into the events and people who shaped your community, adding layers of meaning to the familiar streets and structures you thought you knew well.

Engaging with the wealth of resources available locally can transform your everyday environment into a playground of learning and leisure. Each visit to a museum, each hike through a park, and each festival attended not only adds vibrancy to your life but also deepens your connection to your community, enriching your retirement with continuous learning and new experiences.

2.2 The Joy of Voluntourism: Combining Travel with Giving Back

Voluntourism, a blend of volunteering and tourism, offers a unique opportunity to enrich your travel experiences by contributing to projects that positively impact local communities. This concept allows you to immerse yourself in new cultures and landscapes while making meaningful contributions to education, conservation, and health. Imagine helping to build a school in a remote village or participating in wildlife conservation efforts; these activities provide help where needed and offer a connection to the places you visit.

When searching for voluntourism opportunities, it's crucial to choose organizations that are reputable and align with your personal values and interests. Start by researching organizations facilitating these trips, focusing on those that transparently discuss where contributions go and how they impact the community. Websites of non-profit organizations, travel forums, and reviews by previous volunteers are excellent resources for gaining insights into the organization's operations and reputation. It's also important to consider the cost and duration of voluntourism trips, ensuring they fit within your budget and available time. Some organizations might also offer grants or subsidized travel expenses, which can make these experiences more accessible.

Preparing for a voluntourism trip involves practical and cultural considerations to ensure you contribute positively and respectfully. Understanding the community's culture, language, and needs is essential. Engaging in preliminary research or participating in pre-trip orientations offered by the volunteering organization can provide valuable insights into the community's customs and what to expect during your stay. Packing is another critical aspect, where essentials might vary depending on the destination and the nature of the work. For instance, durable clothing and protective footwear are necessary if you're involved in outdoor activities, such as building homes or planting trees. Always consider the local weather and cultural norms when selecting your attire.

The benefits of engaging in voluntourism extend beyond the tangible contributions to the projects. Emotionally, helping others can significantly enhance your sense of purpose and satisfaction. Many volunteers report a profound connection to the people and places they help, often experiencing renewed gratitude and perspective on their lives. Socially, voluntourism provides an opportunity to meet and work alongside people worldwide, fostering friendships and collaborations that can last a lifetime. These experiences can provide memories, skills, and knowledge transferable to other life areas.

As you explore the possibilities of voluntourism, remember that your contributions can significantly impact the communities you visit, no matter how small they seem. This form of travel broadens your horizons and allows you to leave a positive footprint behind, making it a truly fulfilling way to experience the world. Whether you're teaching, building, or conserving, your efforts in voluntourism can transform your travel into an adventure of giving and learning, enriching both your life and those of others.

2.3 Hobby Groups and Clubs: Finding Like-Minded Communities

The richness of retirement can be greatly enhanced by engaging with groups that share your interests, whether it is gardening, reading, or cycling. Finding these groups can help you fill your days with enjoyable activities and connect you with individuals who share similar passions. Local community centers often serve as a hub for various clubs and may offer scheduled meetings for different hobbies. Additionally, libraries frequently host book clubs, craft groups, or historical societies that welcome new members. Attending local exhibitions or fairs related to your hobby can also be a fantastic way to meet informal groups or individuals with similar interests. These events often feature club booths and can provide direct contacts for club organizers. Another effective way to find local groups is through bulletin boards in shops that cater to specific hobbies, like a local nursery for gardeners or a sports shop for cycling enthusiasts.

As previously discussed, technology also plays a pivotal role in connecting like-minded individuals. Platforms such as Meetup or Facebook Groups are excellent resources for finding existing groups or starting your own. Meetup allows you to search for groups by keywords relating to your interests and filter results based on your location. This platform lists various groups ranging from technology workshops to outdoor adventures. It provides details about upcoming events, making it easy to join in on activities that catch your eye. Facebook Groups is another dynamic platform for joining groups dedicated to specific hobbies or interests. These groups often share resources, organize events, and facilitate discussions, providing a virtual community that is accessible from anywhere. Engaging with these online platforms can significantly broaden your social network and lead to friendships and learning opportunities that enrich your retirement life.

Starting your own hobby group can be equally rewarding, especially if existing groups do not meet your specific needs or interests. Begin by defining the group's focus, whether it's a book club, a photography group, or a bird-watching society. Once you have a clear idea, invite a few friends or acquaintances who share your interest to help with the planning. Utilizing local community centers, libraries, or even cafes for meeting spaces can help keep costs low while providing a convenient location for members. Promotion is vital in attracting members, so consider creating flyers to post in relevant local businesses or community boards. Online platforms like Facebook or Nextdoor can also effectively reach a wider audience. Maintaining a regular schedule and varying the activities or discussion topics as your group grows can keep the group engaging and dynamic.

The benefits of participating in hobby groups extend beyond just learning new skills or enjoying a hobby. Social interactions in these settings can significantly enhance your psychological well-being, providing a sense of community and belonging that is crucial in retirement. Sharing knowledge and experiences with those with similar interests can lead to greater appreciation of your hobby. Regular engagements with group members can also keep your social skills and mind active, contributing to overall mental health. The joy of connecting with others who share your passions can transform your retirement into an exciting phase of life filled with friendships, learning, and fun.

Engaging with hobby groups and clubs opens a world of opportunities for personal growth and social interaction. Whether you join an existing group or start your own, the connections you make and the experiences you share can significantly enhance the quality of your retirement, filling your days with joy and purpose.

2.4 DIY Home Projects: Enhancing Your Living Space on a Budget

Retirement offers the perfect opportunity to transform your living space into a reflection of your personal taste and creativity without needing a hefty budget. Engaging in DIY projects not only personalizes your home but also brings the satisfaction of creation and the joy of accomplishment. For instance, repainting old furniture can breathe new life into your rooms, turning a faded chair or table into a vibrant centerpiece. This task requires basic supplies like sandpaper, paint, and brushes, all available at local hardware stores. Choosing a color that complements your decor can unify a room or become an accent piece that sparks conversation. Sanding down the old paint, applying a fresh coat, and watching the transformation is an immensely gratifying and creative expression of your style.

Creating photo frames is another simple yet profoundly personal DIY project. With some basic wood molding, a saw, glue, and your choice of paint or stain, you can create beautiful, custom frames that showcase your cherished memories. This project adds personality to your home decor and allows you to relive and display those special moments. For a simpler version, consider refurbishing old frames with new paint or decorative elements such as beads or fabric. When choosing photos to frame, this activity can be delightful and meaningful, leading to a lovely afternoon reminiscing over old photos and the stories they tell.

Another project that combines functionality with creativity is making homemade candles. This can be done by melting wax—available in craft stores—and adding your scents and colors. Pouring the wax into molds or repurposed containers like teacups or jars creates unique candles that light up your home or serve as thoughtful, handmade gifts for friends and family. Choosing scents can also be a sensory pleasure, and experimenting with combinations like lavender and vanilla or citrus and mint can be an exciting creative outlet.

Gardening Projects: Enhancing Your Space and Well-being

Gardening is a leisurely and productive activity that beautifies your home and provides fresh produce or delightful scents. Starting a small herb garden is an excellent project for both experienced gardeners and novices. Herbs such as basil, mint, and thyme are easy to grow and maintain, making them perfect for a kitchen windowsill or balcony. The convenience of having fresh herbs on hand for cooking is matched by the aromatic pleasure and the lush greenery they add to your home. For those with more space, building a birdhouse can attract wildlife to your garden, creating a lively atmosphere and providing the joy of watching birds visit throughout the seasons. Birdhouses can be made from scrap wood and simple tools and decorating them can be a fun activity that adds a personal touch to your garden.

Resourceful Use of Materials: Creative Repurposing

Resourcefulness is at the heart of DIY projects, especially when repurposing old materials. An old ladder, for example, can be transformed into a charming bookshelf with some cleaning, perhaps a coat of paint, and securing it horizontally or vertically against a wall. The rungs serve as natural shelves for books, plants, or decorative items, blending functionality with rustic charm. Similarly, glass jars from your kitchen can be reused as plant pots, candle holders, or storage containers. Decorating these jars with paints, fabrics, or ribbons can turn everyday objects into art pieces, reducing waste while enhancing your home's aesthetics.

Organizational Hacks: Streamlined Living

Organizing your home effectively can impact your daily comfort and efficiency. Budget-friendly storage solutions can help declutter your living spaces, making them more pleasant and functional. For example, installing shelves in underutilized spaces like under stairs or above door frames can offer extra storage without compromising floor space. Similarly, drawer dividers in your kitchen or bedroom can assist with organization. These small changes can make a big difference in how you enjoy and use your home, making daily routines smoother and your environment more serene.

Engaging in these DIY projects enhances your living space. It offers enjoyable and fulfilling activities you can embark on and enjoy throughout your retirement. Each project adds beauty and functionality to your home, providing a sense of achievement and the pleasure of continual learning and creativity.

2.5 Cooking Classes Online: Learn New Culinary Skills

The art of cooking nourishes not only the body but also the soul. Engaging in cooking classes online can transform your culinary skills and bring the joy of cooking into your home. The internet has abundant resources that make learning to cook accessible and enjoyable. Platforms like YouTube are treasure troves of culinary knowledge where professional chefs and seasoned home cooks share their expertise through detailed tutorials. From mastering the basics like how to properly chop vegetables to more complex tasks like crafting a perfect soufflé, these free resources are invaluable. Additionally, numerous cooking blogs are dedicated to teaching culinary skills and offering recipe guides catering to various dietary preferences and cuisines. These blogs often include step-by-step instructions, photos, and sometimes videos, making it easy to follow at your own pace.

As you explore the vast culinary content, consider starting with simple recipes with everyday ingredients. This approach not only eases you into cooking but also helps build your confidence as you see and taste your successes. Once comfortable, gradually introduce more exotic recipes and techniques, expanding your culinary repertoire. Remember, the goal is to enjoy the process as much as the results. Cooking can be a delightful journey of flavors and discovery that enhances your daily meals and special occasions.

Online cooking classes that offer real-time interaction with instructors add to the learning. These classes, often available on platforms like MasterClass or Udemy, provide a structured learning experience where you can receive immediate feedback and ask questions just as you would in a physical classroom. The real-time aspect fosters a more engaging and interactive learning environment, making it easier to grasp complex cooking techniques. Many of these platforms offer a selection of free classes or trial periods, making them accessible regardless of your budget. Participating in these classes will teach you new recipes and the science behind cooking techniques, which is fundamental for becoming a proficient cook.

Cooking also offers a beautiful opportunity to connect with others, making it a social activity that can be enjoyed with friends and family, even if they are not physically present. Organizing virtual cook-alongs is a fantastic way to share the experience. You could select a recipe, set a date, and invite friends or family members to cook the same meal simultaneously while connected through a video call. This activity makes the cooking process more enjoyable and helps maintain social connections. Sharing tips and personal tweaks to recipes during these sessions can lead to lively conversations and a shared meal experience despite the physical distance.

Moreover, the benefits of cooking at home extend beyond just the pleasure of eating good food. Preparing meals at home allows you to control the quality of ingredients and the cooking methods, contributing to better health. Opting for fresh, locally sourced ingredients can enhance the nutritional benefits of your meals. Economically, home cooking is also more cost-effective than dining out regularly. By planning and preparing your meals, you can manage your food budget more efficiently, reducing waste and maximizing your available resources. Planning meals and cooking can also provide a structured yet creative routine that enhances your daily life, offering satisfaction beyond the dinner table.

In embracing the world of online cooking, you are not just learning to make delicious dishes; you are also adopting a lifestyle that promotes better health, creativity, and social connectivity. Whether you are a novice in the culinary arts or a seasoned cook looking to refine your skills, online resources provide a rich, accessible, and fulfilling way to engage with cooking. Each recipe tried and each skill mastered not only adds to your culinary ability but also brings a sense of accomplishment and joy, enriching your life one dish at a time.

2.6 Free Online Entertainment Resources: Movies, Books, and Games

The digital age has ushered in many opportunities to access entertainment without leaving the comfort of your home or spending a dime. Public libraries, a long-valued resource for communities, have expanded their services to the digital realm, providing more than just physical books. Through apps like OverDrive and Hoopla, libraries offer free access to a vast collection of eBooks, audiobooks, and movies. You'll need a library card from your local library to start using these services. Once you have your card, download the app on your tablet, smartphone, or computer and log in using your library credentials. You can then browse and borrow digital media like a physical book. These platforms usually have user-friendly interfaces that make searching for specific titles or exploring new genres relatively straightforward. Moreover, they often feature recommendation systems that suggest books or films based on your borrowing history, enhancing your experience and discovering new interests.

Several free streaming services offer various options for those who enjoy visual entertainment. Platforms like Crackle and Tubi provide free access to thousands of movies and TV shows. These services are supported by ads, which means you can watch without a subscription fee. Both platforms are easy to navigate and available on various devices, including smart TVs, streaming devices, and mobile phones, making watching your favorite shows or discovering new ones from anywhere convenient. Each service offers an eclectic mix of genres, ensuring something to pique everyone's interest, whether it's a classic movie, a romantic comedy, or a thrilling documentary.

The internet is also fantastic for those who enjoy puzzles and games. Websites like Pogo and Miniclip offer a wide range of free games, from classic card and board games to more complex puzzle games and trivia contests. These platforms also allow you to play against opponents worldwide or set up private sessions with friends and family. Engaging in these games can be an excellent way to keep your mind sharp, as many are designed to challenge cognitive functions like memory, strategy, and problem-solving skills.

Virtual book clubs have become a significant social outlet for many, especially when meeting in person is not feasible. These clubs can be found through social media platforms like Facebook, where groups are formed and managed, or through websites dedicated to readers, such as Goodreads. These platforms allow you to join existing clubs or start your own, discussing your latest read with others who share your passion for literature. Participating in a virtual book club enriches your reading experience through discussion and diverse perspectives. It helps maintain social connections, fostering community and shared interest. These digital resources enhance your leisure time and connect you with broader communities and new experiences. The accessibility of free digital media ensures that entertainment and learning can continue unabated, regardless of physical or financial limitations. As you explore these options, you embrace the joy of entertainment and the continuing journey of lifelong learning and connection.

CHAPTER 3
PHYSICAL HEALTH AND WELLNESS

As you continue to navigate the enriching path of retirement, maintaining your physical health becomes a gateway to enjoying this vibrant chapter of life to its fullest. Think of your body as a well-loved vehicle that has served you faithfully; it now deserves attentive maintenance and caring upgrades.

3.1 Gentle Yoga for Seniors: Poses for Flexibility and Balance

Introduction to Gentle Yoga

Gentle yoga is a soothing balm for the body's aches and a nurturing embrace for the soul. Tailored specifically for seniors, this form of yoga emphasizes slower movements, softer stretches, and a deep connection with the breath, making it accessible regardless of your fitness level or mobility. Unlike more vigorous styles of yoga, gentle yoga focuses on releasing tension, improving circulation, and enhancing overall flexibility without straining muscles or joints. The practice is often combined with mindful breathing techniques that help foster relaxation and mental clarity. Whether you want to alleviate stiffness from your joints or seek a moment of tranquility in your day, gentle yoga can be adapted to suit your needs, offering a customizable practice that respects your body's limits and celebrates its capabilities.

Key Poses for Seniors

Two foundational poses in gentle yoga are the Tree Pose and the Seated Forward Bend, each serving unique purposes in enhancing your physical balance and flexibility. To begin with the Tree Pose, stand with your feet hip-width apart, grounding yourself firmly. Gently lift your right foot and place the sole against your left inner thigh or calf, avoiding the knee area for safety. Bring your hands together in front of your chest in a prayer position and focus your gaze to maintain balance. Hold this pose for several breaths, then switch to the other leg. This pose enhances your balance and strengthens your legs and core, which is crucial for preventing falls.

The Seated Forward Bend, on the other hand, is performed seated on the floor with legs extended forward. Inhale deeply, and as you exhale, hinge at the hips and lean forward from your lower back, reaching your hands towards your toes. It's not about how far you go—what matters is feeling the stretch along your spine and the back of your legs. This pose helps lengthen your spine, stretch your hamstrings, and promote flexibility. Both poses are not just physical exercises; they are opportunities to connect with your body and appreciate its capacity at this moment.

Benefits of Regular Practice

Incorporating gentle yoga into your daily routine brings a plethora of health benefits. Regular practice can significantly improve joint health, reducing the pain and stiffness associated with conditions such as arthritis. The stretches and poses enhance your flexibility, which can diminish naturally with age, thus improving your overall mobility. Moreover, the meditative aspect of yoga reduces stress and anxiety, promoting a calm, clear mind. These mental benefits are just as vital as the physical ones, as they contribute to a holistic sense of well-being that can enhance your quality of life in profound ways.

Setting Up a Safe Practice Space

Setting up an appropriate space is essential to ensure safety while practicing yoga at home. Begin by choosing a quiet corner of your home where you can practice undisturbed. Place a non-slip yoga mat on the floor to provide cushioning and prevent slipping. If balance is a concern, have a sturdy chair to hold onto for support, or practice near a wall. Ensure the area is clutter-free and has enough space to stretch your arms and legs during various poses. Comfortable clothing allowing for easy movement is essential, as it ensures that your practice is focused solely on your well-being, free from distractions or discomfort.

Gentle yoga offers a beautiful, low-impact way to maintain physical health and enhance mental well-being. By embracing this practice, you care for your body and create moments of peace and reflection in your everyday life, enriching your retirement years with grace and vitality. As you explore these gentle movements and begin to feel their benefits, you may find that yoga becomes an essential part of your routine.

3.2 Aqua Aerobics: A Low-Impact Exercise for Fitness

Aqua aerobics, also known as water aerobics, presents a delightful and effective way for seniors like yourself to stay active while minimizing the risk of injury. Unlike traditional aerobic exercises performed on land, aqua aerobics takes advantage of water's natural buoyancy, significantly reducing the impact on joints. This makes it an ideal exercise for those who experience discomfort during more high-impact activities. Water resistance makes your muscles work harder, providing a solid workout that improves cardiovascular health, enhances muscle strength, and increases flexibility without gravity's harsh impact.

One of the most popular forms of aqua aerobics is water walking. Simply start walking in the pool's shallow end to perform water walking. The water level should be somewhere between your waist and chest. Eventually, you can increase the intensity by moving to deeper water or quickening your pace. Another effective exercise is aqua jogging, which is like water walking but at a faster, more intense pace. Both exercises promote cardiovascular health, strengthen the lower body, and improve endurance. For those looking to increase upper body strength, incorporating arm movements in the water, such as arm circles or using water weights, can provide additional resistance. These activities keep your body physically engaged and ensure that your exercise routine remains varied and enjoyable.

Finding a suitable class that caters to your needs and preferences is critical to integrating aqua aerobics into your life. Many local gyms, community centers, and YMCAs offer aqua aerobics classes designed specifically for seniors. These classes accommodate various fitness levels and often focus on gentle movements that are safe yet effective. To locate a class near you, check the schedules at local aquatic centers or community pools. Many of these facilities have websites with detailed information about the classes they offer, including descriptions, times, and levels of intensity. Don't hesitate to call or visit to ask questions about the class structure and the instructor's experience, particularly with senior participants. You must feel comfortable and safe in the class environment to enjoy the benefits fully. Safety in the water is paramount, especially when dealing with physical activities that could pose risks if not performed correctly.

When participating in aqua aerobics, it's crucial to use proper equipment. Water weights, which are lightweight and designed for underwater use, can help enhance resistance and build muscle strength without straining your body.

Similarly, noodles and kickboards can be used for various exercises, aiding balance and providing support during different movements. It's also important to wear water shoes to prevent slipping and to provide your feet with extra protection and traction. Before starting any exercise, warm up with gentle stretches or a light walk in the water to prepare your muscles and joints. This reduces the risk of injury. Always listen to your body and avoid movements that cause pain or discomfort, ensuring your aqua aerobics experience is beneficial and enjoyable.

Incorporating aqua aerobics into your fitness routine is a great way to enhance your physical health while also enjoying the soothing benefits of being in the water. The supportive environment of the water, combined with the camaraderie found in group classes, can also contribute to your emotional and social well-being, making aqua aerobics a holistic approach to maintaining health and vitality during retirement. Whether you're just beginning to explore fitness options suitable for your lifestyle or looking to add variety to your existing routine, aqua aerobics offers a refreshing way to accomplish your health goals while having fun in the water. As you continue to engage in these water-based exercises, you may find a renewed sense of energy and a greater capacity to enjoy all the activities you love, both in and out of the water.

3.3 Walking Clubs: Socializing While Staying Fit

The simple act of walking, often underestimated, unfolds numerous benefits, particularly when shared in the camaraderie of a walking club. These clubs bolster your physical health through regular exercise and enrich your social life, connecting you with peers who share a zest for active living. Walking together in a group can transform a solitary activity into an engaging social event where each step contributes to your physical well-being and fosters meaningful relationships. The rhythmic pace of walking allows for conversations ranging from light-hearted chats to deeper discussions, making each session something to look forward to. Moreover, walking in a group can enhance your motivation, turning exercise into a pleasant routine rather than a chore and providing a mutual support system that encourages regular participation.

For those interested in joining a walking club, local community centers, senior centers, and health clubs often sponsor these groups. These organizations typically understand the needs and preferences of seniors, ensuring that the walking routes and paces are suitable for older adults. Additionally, websites like Meetup.com can help locate walking groups in your area. These platforms allow you to search by interests and location, providing an easy way to find a group that matches your fitness level and walking preferences. If there isn't an existing club that meets your needs, consider starting one. Begin by inviting friends or neighbors for regular walks. Use community bulletin boards, social media, or local community newsletters to advertise your new club. Consistency is critical when organizing a walking club; set regular days and times for walks and plan routes in advance to keep members informed and engaged.

Safety and scenery are paramount when selecting routes for your walking club, especially to ensure an enjoyable experience for all members. Ideal paths are flat, have a minimal incline, are well-paved, and are free from high traffic. Parks, nature reserves, and dedicated walking trails are excellent choices as they provide safe environments and are aesthetically pleasing, making your walks more enjoyable. Consider the length of the route as well; starting with shorter distances and gradually increasing as the group's fitness levels improve can help maintain enthusiasm and prevent injuries. Accessibility is also important, so look for accessible routes, parking facilities, and perhaps even benches along the way for rest stops. Seasonal changes can make specific routes more appealing or appropriate, such as shaded paths for summer or sheltered routes in cooler weather, adding variety to your walking sessions throughout the year.

Incorporating wellness goals within the club can significantly enhance the health benefits of your walking routine. Setting collective goals such as step counts, distance targets, or durations can foster a spirit of friendly competition and achievement among members. Personal pedometers or fitness trackers can monitor individual progress, providing motivation and an accomplishment as goals are met. Additionally, celebrate milestones as a group, whether reaching a step goal, increasing the walking distance, or commemorating the club's anniversaries. These celebrations not only acknowledge the achievements but also strengthen the sense of community within the club.

Encouraging members to share their personal milestones and health improvements can also inspire others, reinforcing the positive impact of the club on their overall well-being.

Walking clubs offer a wonderful blend of health promotion and social interaction, making them a perfect activity for seniors seeking to enhance their lifestyle. By combining exercise with social engagement, these clubs create a supportive community that motivates its members to maintain active and fulfilling lives. As you step out with your walking club, each walk becomes more than just physical activity; it becomes a shared experience that enriches your health, happiness, and social connections.

3.4 Tai Chi: Exploring Its Benefits for Mental and Physical Health

Tai Chi, an ancient Chinese martial art, is often described as meditation in motion and is particularly well-suited to your pace and needs as a senior. Unlike some forms of exercise that emphasize vigorous aerobic movement, Tai Chi focuses on slow, deliberate movements, deep breathing, and mental concentration. Originating from ancient China, this practice has evolved over centuries, embodying principles of tranquility and peace. The beauty of Tai Chi lies in its adaptability; it can be modified to suit your physical capabilities while still providing profound health benefits. Its gentle nature makes it an ideal exercise for maintaining strength, flexibility, and balance as you age.

Learning the core movements and routines of Tai Chi can significantly enhance your physical stability and flexibility. One fundamental aspect of Tai Chi is the form, a series of movements executed slowly, focused, and accompanied by deep breathing. Each posture transitions into the next without pause, ensuring your body is in constant motion. For instance, the 'Wave Hands like Clouds' move involves soft, sweeping motions with the arms, which enhance upper body flexibility and coordination. Another common sequence, 'Brush Knee and Push,' combines a lunge with a simultaneous hand motion, promoting balance and lower body strength. These movements are not only physical exercises but also deeply meditative practices that help center your mind, encouraging a state of mental calm and clarity.

The mental health benefits of Tai Chi are as significant as the physical ones. Regular practice has been shown to reduce stress and anxiety, thanks to its meditative nature. The focus on breath and movement can help quiet the mind, offering a break from the hustle of daily life. This mindfulness aspect encourages a greater awareness of the present moment, a powerful tool for emotional well-being. Moreover, Tai Chi has been linked to improved mood and better cognitive function. This practice can help sharpen your mental faculties, enhance your memory, and provide a sense of overall well-being. These qualities make Tai Chi not just a physical exercise but a holistic approach to maintaining your health at a higher standard.

Finding resources to learn Tai Chi is easier than you think, offering flexibility in how and where you practice. Many community centers, senior centers, and local gyms offer Tai Chi classes, which are often tailored to the needs of older adults. These classes provide the added benefit of a social environment, allowing you to connect with peers while engaging in physical activity. If you prefer to learn at home, numerous online resources can guide you through the basics of Tai Chi. Websites like YouTube have channels dedicated to Tai Chi instruction with videos that allow you to progress at your own pace. Additionally, instructional DVDs can be purchased online or borrowed from your local library, providing detailed guidance through various Tai Chi routines that you can follow from the comfort of your home. These resources make it easy to integrate this gentle yet effective form of exercise into your daily routine, helping you maintain mobility and mental sharpness.

Through Tai Chi, you gain more than just a physical workout; you embark on a path that encompasses holistic health benefits, enhancing your life in multiple dimensions. As you continue to practice and delve deeper into the art of Tai Chi, you may find a profound sense of peace and fulfillment, enriching your experience of your golden years. With each movement and breath, Tai Chi offers a way to reclaim your space, find your pace, and appreciate every moment with renewed vigor and calm.

3.5 Home Fitness Routines: Exercises That Don't Require Equipment

Maintaining a regular exercise routine at home can be convenient and comforting, especially when you have a plan that balances stretching, strength-building, and cardiovascular activities. Designing an effective home workout routine doesn't require expensive equipment or a lot of space; instead, it involves selecting activities you enjoy that meet your health needs. The beauty of home workouts lies in their flexibility—you can tailor them to fit your schedule, preferences, and fitness level, making it easier to stick to a routine consistently.

Start by considering the layout of your typical week. Allocating specific days and times for your workouts can establish a routine, making it more likely that you'll stick to it. For example, you may dedicate 30 minutes to exercise every morning or perhaps an hour every other day, depending on what works best for you. It's also helpful to vary the types of exercises you do throughout the week to ensure a balanced approach that enhances all aspects of your fitness. For instance, focus on stretching and flexibility exercises like dynamic stretching or Pilates on Mondays and Wednesdays, dedicate Tuesdays and Thursdays to strength-building exercises, and reserve Fridays for a more extended session that includes cardiovascular activities like brisk walking or dancing.

Incorporating no-equipment exercises into your routine is a cost-effective way to enhance your strength and flexibility while improving cardiovascular health. Chair exercises, for example, are fantastic for those who may have balance concerns or prefer a more supported workout. These can include seated marches, where you lift your knees alternately as high as possible, or chair stands, which involve sitting and standing repeatedly to strengthen leg muscles. Wall push-ups are another excellent choice for building upper body strength without needing weights. Simply stand an arm's length from a wall, place your hands flat against it, and slowly bend your elbows to bring your chest towards the wall before pushing back to the starting position. Leg lifts, another effective strength exercise, can be performed lying down or standing and involves lifting your legs to the front, side, and back to enhance lower body strength.

Ensuring your routine caters to your specific fitness level is crucial. All exercises can be modified to increase or decrease their intensity. For instance, if you find standard wall push-ups too easy, you can increase the difficulty by stepping further away from the wall, which requires more strength to push back up. Conversely, if you find them too challenging, standing closer to the wall will reduce the strain. Similarly, with leg lifts, using ankle weights can add extra resistance as your strength improves, or you can perform the lifts more slowly to increase the challenge without additional equipment. Listening to your body is key; adjust the intensity of your workouts based on how you feel and any specific health concerns you might have.

Creating a home workout routine allows you to maintain your physical health on your own terms. By carefully selecting and scheduling exercises, you ensure your routine is balanced and enjoyable, increasing the likelihood of long-term adherence. Furthermore, adapting exercises to suit your fitness level allows you to challenge yourself safely as your strength and endurance grow. This approach helps maintain your physical health and enhances your independence and quality of life by keeping you active and engaged in your daily activities.

3.6 Nutrition Over 60: Eating Well for Longevity

As we age, our bodies undergo various changes that can significantly impact our nutritional needs. Understanding these changes is crucial to maintaining your health and enhancing your quality of life during your golden years. One of the most significant changes is the need to increase certain nutrients like calcium, vitamin D, and fiber intake. Calcium and vitamin D are essential for maintaining bone health, which is critical as bone density tends to decrease in older adults, increasing the risk of fractures. Vitamin D is vital for bone health, supporting the immune system, and reducing inflammation. Fiber, on the other hand, plays a crucial role in digestive health, helping to prevent constipation, which can be a common issue as you age. It also helps to regulate blood sugar levels and can aid in maintaining a healthy weight.

A balanced diet rich in fruits, vegetables, lean proteins, and whole grains can help you meet these nutritional needs. Fruits and vegetables are high in vitamins, minerals, and antioxidants, essential for combating age-related oxidative stress and inflammation. Aim to fill half of your plate with fruits and vegetables at each meal, focusing on various colors to ensure a wide range of nutrients. Lean proteins such as chicken, fish, beans, and legumes are essential for muscle repair and maintenance. As metabolism slows with age, maintaining muscle mass through adequate protein intake can help manage weight and reduce the risk of chronic diseases. Whole grains, such as brown rice, whole wheat, oats, and barley, provide the necessary fiber to support digestive health and prevent chronic conditions like type 2 diabetes and heart disease.

Meal planning and preparation can be a great way to ensure you're eating nutritious and balanced meals. Start by creating a weekly meal plan that includes a variety of foods to cover all the food groups. This not only helps with efficient shopping but also reduces food waste. Keep your kitchen stocked with foods such as whole grains, lean proteins, dairy products, and fresh or frozen fruits and vegetables. Preparing meals in batches can save time and ensure you have healthy options on hand, especially on days when cooking feels like too much effort. Simple cooking methods such as steaming, grilling, or baking are not only easy but also preserve the nutritional content of food better than frying or lengthy cooking processes.

Hydration is another crucial aspect of nutrition for seniors, yet it is often overlooked. As you age, your body's ability to conserve water decreases and you may experience decreased sense of thirst. These changes can increase the risk of dehydration, which can exacerbate many health issues, including kidney problems and cardiovascular disorders. Incorporating water-rich foods like cucumbers, tomatoes, oranges, and melons into your diet can also help boost your hydration. Herbal teas and broth-based soups are other enjoyable ways to increase fluid intake while also providing nourishment.

In summary, adapting your diet to meet the changing nutritional needs of aging is key to sustaining your health and vitality. By emphasizing the intake of crucial nutrients, incorporating a variety of healthful foods, and focusing on proper hydration, you can significantly enhance your overall well-being. As you integrate these nutritional strategies into your daily life, you'll find that eating well can be both enjoyable and beneficial, supporting your journey through the golden years with strength and vigor.

As we conclude this chapter on maintaining physical health and wellness, it's clear that a combination of balanced nutrition, regular exercise, and mindful practices like yoga and Tai Chi can significantly enhance your quality of life. These elements keep your body in optimal health and enrich your daily experiences, allowing you to enjoy your retirement to the fullest.

CHAPTER 4
MENTAL ENGAGEMENT AND LIFELONG LEARNING

Like a fine wine, the mind can improve with age, given the right development opportunities. Embracing mental engagement as a fundamental aspect of your retirement can transform this period into one of the most intellectually fruitful times of your life. Imagine this chapter of your life as a grand library, where every book represents a potential new skill, hobby, or knowledge waiting to be discovered. This chapter explores the joys and immense benefits of keeping your mind as active as your body, ensuring a well-rounded and fulfilling retirement.

4.1 Brain Games: Keep Your Mind Sharp with Puzzles and Quizzes

Introduction to Cognitive Games

Maintaining mental agility as we get older is essential not only for our cognitive functions but also for our overall happiness and quality of life. Cognitive exercises are a delightful and effective way to fine-tune your mind, like tuning a piano to ensure it plays every note with clarity and precision. These activities help relieve cognitive decline and enhance memory, focus, and problem-solving skills. Engaging regularly in brain games is akin to sending your brain to the gym, where each mental workout increases strength and agility.

Types of Brain Games

Brain games are a broad category that includes a variety of puzzles and quizzes designed to challenge different aspects of cognitive function. Crosswords and Sudoku, for example, are fantastic for improving your problem-solving skills and ability to recognize patterns. These games can be found in daily newspapers, online, or in dedicated puzzle books available in most bookstores. Memory games, another popular type of brain game, help to enhance memory capabilities. These can be as simple as remembering a list of words and recalling them an hour later or more structured, like memory matching games on apps and websites designed to test cognitive abilities.

Interactive brain game apps such as Lumosity or Peak offer a wide range of cognitive challenges scientifically designed to boost various aspects of brain function. These platforms use the latest neuroscience research to create fun and engaging games that adapt in difficulty as your abilities improve, providing a personalized brain training experience. Most apps offer a free version with subscription options for a more comprehensive feature set, making them accessible regardless of budget.

Setting a Routine

Incorporating brain games into your routine can help you build and maintain cognitive resilience. Start with setting aside a specific time each day for these activities—perhaps in the morning with your coffee or as an evening ritual before bedtime. Consistency is vital; regular mental stimulation is crucial for the games to benefit your brain health. Begin with sessions as short as 15 minutes and gradually increase the amount of time as your concentration improves. It's important to keep this practice enjoyable and not overly challenging at first to encourage daily habit formation.

Tracking Progress

Tracking your progress is essential to keep your cognitive exercises rewarding and motivating. Many brain game apps offer progress tracking as part of their features, providing reports and graphs showing how your skills improve over time. These insights can be incredibly satisfying, showing tangible proof of your mental improvements. For games not tracked by apps, consider keeping a simple journal where you note down the types of puzzles you complete and any improvements you notice, such as faster completion times or advancing to more complex puzzles. Seeing your progress can be a powerful motivator for you to keep engaging with these brain-boosting activities.

Engaging regularly in cognitive exercises enriches your life by keeping your mind sharp and responsive. As you explore the vast array of brain games available and make them a regular part of your life, you'll maintain your cognitive capabilities and discover the joy of continuously learning and adapting. This mental agility will serve you well in all aspects of life, making every day a challenge and a pleasure to navigate.

4.2 Book Clubs: Discover New Genres and Authors

Book clubs offer a delightful way to enrich your retirement years, providing intellectual stimulation and a social setting to share and discuss a wide range of literary works. Suppose you're contemplating starting your own book club or joining an existing one. In that case, there are several key considerations to ensure the experience is as rewarding as possible. Your local library can be an excellent resource for starting a book club. Many libraries host book clubs as part of their community outreach programs, and they often manage multiple groups that cater to various interests and demographics, including specific clubs for seniors. These library-hosted clubs can be especially appealing if you're seeking a group that meets regularly in a familiar, accessible setting.

Starting your own book club involves a few simple steps but requires enthusiasm and a bit of organization. Begin by deciding the focus of your club—do you want to explore classic literature, dive into historical novels, or keep up with contemporary bestsellers? Once you've set a theme, invite friends or acquaintances who share your interest in this genre. You can also advertise your new club at your local library, community center or online through social media platforms like Facebook or Nextdoor to attract members from your community. When scheduling your first meeting, choose a public place like a coffee shop, a quiet restaurant, or a community meeting room, which can offer a relaxed and neutral environment for everyone. Establishing ground rules in your first meeting is helpful to ensure discussions remain respectful and enjoyable for all members.

Selecting the right books is crucial to keeping the club engaging and lively. Aim for a diverse selection of genres and authors to cater to varying tastes and to introduce members to new literary realms they might have yet to venture into. Planning a few months in advance is often beneficial, giving members ample time to obtain and read the books. Consider mixing genres and switching between newer and older works to keep the discussions dynamic. Book selection can be a collective process, where each member suggests a book and then the group votes, or it can rotate, with a different member picking a book each month. This method ensures everyone can introduce their favorites and broaden the group's literary horizons.

Organizing discussions for each book is another vital aspect of a successful book club. A good conversation starts with well-thought-out questions that provoke thoughts beyond the plot summary. Ask about the development of characters, the themes explored in the book, or how the setting influenced the story's events. Encouraging members to bring their questions or discussion points can lead to richer conversations. It's also rewarding to relate the book's themes or characters to personal experiences, as this often deepens understanding and enhances connection among group members.

Virtual book clubs are an excellent alternative for those who prefer or require remote participation. These clubs can be found on various online platforms and connect you with book lovers across the globe. If you are setting up a virtual book club, video conferencing tools like Zoom or Google Meet are user-friendly options that allow real-time discussions. When organizing virtual meetings, sending clear instructions on using the chosen platform is essential, ensuring all members can participate without technical difficulties. The virtual format also allows for more flexibility in scheduling, accommodating members with different time constraints.

Participating in a book club, whether physically or virtually, deepens your appreciation for literature and strengthens your social connections. Each book read and discussed opens new avenues of thought and conversation, enriching your life with diverse perspectives and memorable discussions. As you continue to explore new genres and authors through your book club, you'll find that each meeting brings new stories to enjoy and new understandings to ponder, making every gathering a highlight of your month.

4.3 Learning a New Language: Tools and Tips for Beginners

Embarking on the adventure of learning a new language in your golden years is not just about adding a skill; it's about enriching your mind and soul. The cognitive benefits of language learning are well-documented, with studies showing that bilingual individuals tend to have better memory and more robust cognitive functions than their monolingual peers. Engaging with a new language can also stave off cognitive decline and even delay the onset of dementia. Beyond the brain health benefits, learning a language opens incredible avenues for cultural exchange and a deeper understanding of the world, enhancing social interactions and potentially leading to new friendships formed over shared linguistic skills.

When selecting which language to learn, consider your interests, cultural heritage, or practical reasons such as upcoming travels or a community of speakers near you. Suppose you have always been fascinated by French culture, for instance. In that case, learning French will allow you to enjoy French literature and films more profoundly and enhance any trips to France with the ability to interact with locals in their language. Similarly, if you live in an area with a significant Spanish-speaking population, learning Spanish could help you connect better with your community. Reflecting on why you want to learn a particular language will keep you motivated throughout the learning process.

There are numerous resources available to make language learning accessible and enjoyable. Online platforms like Duolingo or Rosetta Stone offer comprehensive programs that guide you through the basics to more advanced levels at your own pace. These platforms use engaging methods such as interactive dialogs, vocabulary games, and pronunciation practice, making the learning process effective and fun. Many community colleges also offer language courses designed for learners of all ages, providing the added benefit of learning in a classroom where you can practice speaking directly with peers and receive guidance from experienced instructors.

Setting realistic goals is crucial in keeping your language learning journey on track. Start with small, achievable objectives, such as learning to introduce yourself or conducting a five-minute conversation in your new language. Celebrate these milestones, no matter how small, as each represents progress. Over time, you can set more ambitious goals, such as understanding a movie without subtitles or reading a book in the language. These goals provide motivation and help measure your progress in practical, enjoyable ways.

Engaging with the language daily, even briefly, is key to retaining what you learn. Try to incorporate the language into your daily routine, such as listening to music, watching news clips, or reading articles in the language you're learning. This immersion will help reinforce your new skills and make learning a natural part of your day. Remember, the goal is to enjoy the process as much as the outcomes, so keep your approach flexible and focused on enjoying every step of your language-learning adventure.

4.4 Creative Writing: Starting Your Memoir

Writing a memoir is not just about preserving memories; it's a profound journey into self-discovery and reflection that offers therapeutic benefits and a lasting legacy. As you embark on this personal project, consider it an opportunity to delve deep into the events that shaped your life, allowing you to understand and appreciate your experiences from a new perspective. This process can provide a sense of closure or acceptance of past events. Furthermore, sharing your life story can be a precious gift to future generations, offering them insights into their heritage and a personal connection to their past.

When you begin to structure your memoir, think of it not just as a chronicle of events but as a narrative that conveys the emotional journey of your life. Start with an outline that highlights key moments you want to cover. This doesn't have to follow a strict chronological order; sometimes, thematic development can be more engaging. For instance, organize your memoir around significant themes such as resilience, love, or discovery, each represented by different phases or events in your life. As you outline, consider where you want to delve deeper into detail and where a broader overview suffices.

Developing a compelling narrative voice is crucial in connecting with your readers, whether they are family members familiar with your story or strangers who find resonance in your experiences. Your voice should be authentic to your personality. Are you naturally humorous? Reflective? Whatever your style, let it come through as you narrate your life. This authenticity makes your memoir more engaging and relatable.

Writing workshops and resources can be incredibly valuable as you craft your memoir. Many community centers, libraries, and online platforms offer writing groups focusing on memoir writing. These groups provide feedback, support, and motivation, which can be crucial as you navigate the personal and sometimes emotional process of writing about your life. Online courses specific to memoir writing can also provide structure and professional guidance. For a more interactive experience, platforms like Meetup.com can help you find local writing groups where you can share your work in a supportive environment and receive constructive feedback. Publishing your memoir is the final step in sharing your story with the world.

For those who want to keep it personal, sharing your memoir through a blog can be a simple and effective way to reach family and friends. Blogs are easy to set up and maintain, allowing you to publish your story chapter by chapter, which can be less daunting than writing a whole book at once. For those looking to reach a broader audience, self-publishing platforms like Amazon's Kindle Direct Publishing or print-on-demand services like Blurb offer the tools to publish your memoir without a traditional publisher. These platforms provide various formatting tools and cover design options, making producing a professional-looking book relatively easy.

Considering these options, remember that your memoir is a unique and valuable testament to your life's journey. Whether shared privately with loved ones or published for a wider audience, your story is a meaningful legacy that captures the essence of your experiences and the lessons they hold. Writing a memoir preserves and celebrates these memories, offering insight and inspiration to all who read it. As you put pen to paper, embrace the opportunity to tell your story honestly and passionately, crafting an enriching and enlightening narrative.

4.5 Art Classes: Painting and Drawing from Home

Embracing your creative side through painting and drawing can be one of the most rewarding and therapeutic ways to spend time during your retirement. Whether you're a seasoned artist or a beginner looking to explore your artistic abilities, setting up a proper space and gathering the right supplies is the first step in your creative journey. The key for those just starting out is to keep things simple and affordable. Basic supplies like sketchbooks, brushes, watercolors, acrylic paints, and some pencils are sufficient. These are readily available at your local arts and crafts store or online, often at reasonable prices. When setting up your space, look for an area in your home with good natural light, which will help you see actual colors and details in your work. A comfortable chair and a sturdy table are also important, as they will support your posture and allow you to focus on your creativity rather than discomfort.

Finding inspiration for your art can come from a multitude of sources. Everyday life offers endless ideas; a bowl of fruit on your table, a scenic view from your window, or even an interesting pattern on a fabric can ignite your artistic imagination. With its vast array of colors and shapes, nature is also a profound source of inspiration. Try walking in your local park or garden and observe the intricate details of leaves and flowers or how light plays on different surfaces. For those who prefer structured inspiration, online art galleries showcasing a variety of styles and mediums can be incredibly stimulating. Websites like DeviantArt or the digital collections of famous museums can offer you a glimpse into different artistic expressions and motivate you to try new techniques or subjects.

Online art tutorials have made learning how to paint or draw more accessible than ever. Platforms like YouTube offer thousands of free tutorials that can guide you step-by-step through different art projects. These tutorials cater to all skill levels and interests, from basic drawing skills to advanced painting techniques. Websites like Skillshare or Udemy provide courses professional artists teach for a more structured approach. These courses often come with a small fee but offer in-depth knowledge and personalized advice through user forums where you can post your work and receive feedback. Engaging with these online resources helps you improve your techniques. It keeps you connected to a global community of learners and creators, providing a sense of belonging and mutual encouragement.

Sharing your artwork with others can be as rewarding as the process of creating it. Social media platforms like Instagram and Pinterest are fantastic places to showcase your work, connect with other artists, and receive feedback. Consider participating in local art fairs or exhibitions if you're more comfortable with in-person interactions. Many communities host events where local artists can display and sell their work, providing an opportunity to engage with fellow artists and art lovers. For a more personal touch, gifting your artwork to family and friends can be incredibly fulfilling. Whether a hand-drawn card or a carefully painted canvas, sharing your art can bring you and the receiver joy, strengthening bonds and creating lasting memories.

As you delve into painting and drawing, remember that the joy of art lies not just in the finished piece but in the process of creation itself. Each brushstroke and pencil mark reflects your perspective and emotions, making each piece uniquely yours. Let this artistic endeavor be a liberating and joyful experience that enhances your retirement, filling your days with color and creativity.

4.6 Music Appreciation: Exploring Classical to Contemporary

Music, a universal language, speaks to the heart and enriches the soul, providing both comfort and excitement. Whether it's the serene melodies of classical music, the rhythmic beats of jazz, or the catchy lyrics of modern pop, each genre offers unique sounds and styles that can enhance your auditory palette. Exploring various music genres broadens your cultural knowledge. It taps into different emotional and cognitive areas of the brain, stimulating mental activity and fostering emotional well-being.

Organizing listening sessions can transform music appreciation into a delightful social event. Consider setting up a music appreciation group among your friends or community members. You can explore different genres, share favorite tracks, and discuss the elements that move you. Whether you meet weekly or monthly, each session can be themed around a particular genre or artist. For instance, one meeting could focus on classical music, listening to and discussing Beethoven's symphonies. At the same time, another could explore jazz, immersing the group in the sultry sounds of the saxophone. These gatherings enrich your understanding of music and strengthen connections with others who share your enthusiasm.

Learning basic music theory can be incredibly rewarding for those interested in understanding the building blocks of music. Resources for beginners are plentiful, with websites like musictheory.net providing free tutorials that cover everything from reading music to understanding chord progressions. Books like "Music Theory for Dummies" are excellent for starting out, offering straightforward explanations and practical examples. Understanding the fundamentals of music theory can deepen your appreciation of music, allowing you to recognize the craftsmanship behind a harmonious melody or a compelling musical arrangement.

Attending live performances offers a visceral experience that recorded music cannot match. Check local event listings for concerts by orchestras, jazz clubs, or pop artists. Many communities offer free or low-cost concerts, providing an accessible live music experience. Additionally, with the rise of digital platforms, virtual concerts have become increasingly popular. Websites like StageIt host live performances that you can enjoy from the comfort of your home. These performances often allow for direct interaction with the musicians, adding a personal touch to the concert experience. When attending any live or virtual concert, pay attention to the nuances of the performance—the musicians' energy, the audience's reaction, and the ambiance of the venue or platform. These elements all contribute to the immersive experience of live music.

By exploring different genres, engaging with music theory, and participating in live and virtual concerts, you enhance your auditory skills and enrich your cultural life. Music opens doors to diverse worlds, each with its unique soundtrack and stories. As you delve into these musical landscapes, you'll find that each note and lyric adds depth and joy to your days, making music a constant and cherished companion in your journey through retirement.

As this chapter on mental engagement and lifelong learning comes to a close, we reflect on the enriching experiences that brain games, book clubs, language learning, creative writing, art, and music bring to our lives. Each activity strengthens our cognitive abilities and connects us to wider communities and cultures, making our retirement years vibrant and fulfilling.

HI THERE!

Thank you for sticking around! I hope you have enjoyed the book so far and are ready to try out some of the new things you have learned.

Your opinion really matters to me, and I'd love to hear what you think about the book. Could you please take a few minutes to write a review? Your review helps others decide if this book is right for them, and it helps me make future books even better.

Here's how you can leave a review:

1. **Go to the Book's Page:** Visit the website where you bought or read this book.
2. **Find the Review Section**: Scroll down to where you can leave a comment or rating.
3. **Share Your Thoughts:** Write a little about what you liked. Did you learn something new? Did you try a fun activity from the book? What part was your favorite?

Your review doesn't have to be lengthy—just a few sentences can make a big difference. Whether you loved the book or have ideas about improving it, I appreciate your honest feedback.

Thank you so much for your time and support. I hope your retirement is filled with joy, fun, and new adventures!

Best wishes,

> **- Neal M. Kenwick,** author of *"Enjoy Retirement: A Simple Guide to Discovering Fun, Satisfaction, and New Adventures in Your Golden Years"*

CHAPTER 5
SOCIAL CONNECTIONS AND COMMUNITY BUILDING

As you glide into the expansive horizon of your retirement, fostering social connections and building community links can dramatically enhance the richness of your daily life. Imagine each social interaction and community tie as a thread in a vibrant tapestry, each adding strength and color to the overall picture of your life.

5.1 Volunteering: Finding Opportunities in Your Community

Identifying Personal Interests

The first step in embarking on a meaningful volunteer journey is to reflect on your passions and skills. What activities ignite your spirit? Perhaps teaching has always been your calling, suggesting a tutoring program might be rewarding. Or maybe a lifelong love for animals could lead you to volunteer at a local shelter. Begin by listing activities that bring you joy or causes that stir your heart. This list will serve as a compass to guide you toward volunteering opportunities that are not just acts of service but are also profoundly fulfilling and enjoyable. Consider your skills as well; for instance, if you have a knack for knitting, you might contribute by making blankets for newborns at your community hospital.

Using Volunteer Matching Services

Once you have a clear idea of your interests and skills, it's time to connect with organizations that can benefit from your passion and expertise. Online platforms like VolunteerMatch provide an excellent starting point. These websites allow you to search for opportunities based on location and interests. Each listing details the organization's mission, the nature of the volunteer work, and the commitment involved, helping you make an informed decision about where to dedicate your time and energy. Local community boards and social media groups can also be valuable resources, offering insights into smaller, community-based initiatives that might be listed outside larger platforms.

Benefits of Volunteering

Volunteering offers profound benefits that extend far beyond the help provided to the community. Volunteering can significantly enhance your sense of belonging and purpose, particularly in retirement when many traditional roles evolve. Volunteering provides a structured way to stay active and socially engaged, connecting you with people with similar interests and values. Moreover, numerous studies have shown that volunteering can improve mental health. It also offers cognitive benefits, keeping your mind engaged and sharp as you organize events, solve problems, and interact with diverse groups of people.

Long-Term Commitments vs. One-Time Events

Choosing between long-term commitments and one-time events depends mainly on your lifestyle and how you prefer to balance your time. Long-term volunteering might involve regular shifts at a local library or committing to a weekly program teaching skills to children. These positions often allow for deeper relationships and a strong community impact. On the other hand, one-time events such as beach clean-ups or charity runs can provide flexibility, allowing you to contribute without a prolonged commitment. These events are perfect for those who enjoy variety or have schedules that require more flexibility. Both types of commitments have their merits, and many find a combination of both best suits their needs and availability.

Volunteering is more than just giving your time; it's a gateway to new friendships, learning opportunities, and the deep satisfaction of knowing you are making a tangible difference in the world. As you step forward to offer your skills and passion, you enhance the lives of others and enrich your own, weaving a pattern of giving and growth that improves the tapestry of your retirement years. Whether you engage in regular volunteering roles or occasional community events, the joy and fulfillment from this service are bound to illuminate your days and give you a profound sense of connection and purpose.

5.2 Joining Senior Centers: Activities and Networking

Senior centers are vibrant activity and social interaction hubs designed to meet the diverse needs and interests of individuals like you, who are in their golden years but still eager to engage fully with life. These centers are not just facilities; they are lively communities offering various programs to enrich your daily routine and connect you with peers with similar interests. To locate a senior center in your area, you might start with a simple internet search for "senior centers near me," or you could visit your local municipality's website, which often lists community resources. Another fruitful approach is asking friends or family members if they recommend local centers. Once you find a center, a visit can provide a wealth of information about the programs they offer and the community you might soon be part of.

At a senior center, you'll discover various activities designed to keep your body and mind engaged. Common offerings include arts and crafts classes, where you can learn new skills like painting, pottery, or knitting. These classes stimulate your creativity and provide a tangible sense of accomplishment as you see your projects come to life. Group fitness classes such as yoga or water aerobics cater to keeping you physically active in a safe, supportive environment. These classes are tailored to different fitness levels. They are a great way to maintain or improve your strength, flexibility, and overall health. Social outings are another exciting feature of senior centers. These could be trips to local museums, concerts, or restaurants, offering you new experiences and the joy of shared adventures with new friends.

Regularly attending a senior center can transform your daily life. It offers a structured, comforting schedule, knowing you have places to go and people to see consistently. This regularity can significantly enhance your sense of belonging and community. Imagine starting your day with a water aerobics class, followed by a coffee break with friends, and finishing with an afternoon of card games or book club discussions. This kind of active schedule keeps you engaged, reduces feelings of loneliness, and can significantly enhance your overall happiness. Moreover, the social interactions you'll enjoy can lead to new, meaningful, supportive friendships, further enriching your life.

Another enriching aspect of senior centers is the opportunity to engage in peer-led groups or committees. These groups often focus on event planning, community outreach, or even center governance. Joining one of these can enhance your leadership skills and give you a voice in the community, allowing you to contribute your ideas and experience in meaningful ways. Whether organizing an event, leading a workshop, or representing the center at community events, these roles can provide a profound sense of purpose and empowerment. Engaging deeply in the center's activities and taking on leadership roles can make your experience at a senior center not just about what you take but also what you give back, creating a balanced and fulfilling engagement with your community.

5.3 Starting a Club: Tips for Creating a Group Based on Interests

Creating a group or club based on shared interests can be a delightful way to bring purpose and joy to your retirement years, offering both social interaction and intellectual stimulation. The initial step in this rewarding endeavor is clearly defining the club's purpose. Whether it's a book club, gardening group, or walking club, understanding and articulating the group's focus helps attract like-minded individuals. Once the purpose is established, the next crucial step is to decide on the frequency and location of meetings. A monthly gathering at a community center or weekly meetups in a member's home? Each option has its merits, and your decision will likely depend on the availability and preferences of the group members. Accessibility is critical, so ensure the chosen venue is convenient for all members, considering transportation, physical accessibility, and parking availability.

Once the logistics are set, attracting members is your next objective. Start by contacting your personal network—friends, family, and acquaintances who might share your interest. Community bulletin boards, both online and in libraries or community centers, can be invaluable for reaching a wider audience. Don't underestimate the power of social media platforms like Facebook or Nextdoor, where local groups can post events and invitations. Word of mouth, however, remains one of the most effective recruitment tools. Encourage friends to bring someone along to the first few meetings, expanding the club's reach through personal connections.

Managing club activities efficiently is crucial to maintaining engagement and ensuring that meetings remain compelling for all members. Begin each meeting with a clear agenda and allocate time for all planned activities. Whether discussing a recent book, sharing gardening tips, or planning a group walk, a structured approach helps keep meetings focused and productive. It's also beneficial to periodically review these activities to ensure they continue to meet the interests of the club members. This might mean introducing new activities or topics occasionally to keep the engagement high.

Sustaining interest in the club over time can be one of the more challenging aspects of running a group. Introducing guest speakers who can provide expert insights on the club's focus area is a fantastic way to inject new energy into meetings. Guest speakers can transform a routine gathering into an exciting event, sparking renewed enthusiasm and providing fresh perspectives. Rotating leadership roles within the club can also keep things lively. When members take turns organizing meetings or leading discussions, they often bring new ideas and styles to the leadership role, keeping the format dynamic and engaging. Exploring new topics and occasionally revisiting the club's purpose and structure can also keep the club relevant and engaging for all members.

Starting and maintaining a club in retirement can vastly enrich your social life, providing regular interaction with peers who share your interests. It's a pursuit that helps keep you intellectually engaged and builds strong, supportive relationships, enhancing the quality of your everyday life. As you continue to develop your club, remember that flexibility and open communication are the keys to creating a thriving and enduring community group.

5.4 Planning Family Reunions: Making Memorable Gatherings

When the time comes to gather the generations together, a family reunion can transform into a treasured event, brimming with laughter, stories, and the rekindling of bonds. As you begin to envision such a gathering, setting clear goals that reflect what you hope to achieve is crucial. Whether it's to celebrate a significant family milestone, such as an important wedding anniversary or a grandparent's milestone birthday, or simply to enjoy each other's company, having a defined objective can guide your planning process and ensure the event meets your expectations. For some, the primary goal might be strengthening family ties, particularly if relatives don't often see one another. In this case, activities encouraging interaction and shared experiences can be particularly beneficial.

Selecting a date and venue that accommodates everyone's schedules and needs is paramount. It often helps to plan months in advance, especially if family members travel from afar. Consider using online polls to propose multiple dates and see which works best for the majority. When choosing a venue, consider accessibility for all family members, including those with mobility issues, and whether the location offers activities and amenities that appeal to various age groups. Renting space at a park with playgrounds and picnic areas or a family-friendly resort offering lodging and entertainment can be ideal. Planning meals that cater to different dietary needs is also essential, and potluck arrangements or catering services can alleviate the pressure of preparing food while ensuring there are options that everyone can enjoy.

Activities that engage all ages are crucial for a successful family reunion. Consider organizing games that children and adults can participate in, like sack races, scavenger hunts, or trivia contests that include questions about family history. Crafts stations where family members can create keepsakes, such as framed family photos or hand-painted ornaments, can also be a hit. For quieter moments, setting up a storytelling corner where the older generations share tales from their youth can captivate listeners and pass down priceless family lore. These activities provide entertainment and foster interactions that can strengthen family relationships and create new memories.

Capturing these moments is equally important, as photos and videos from the reunion will be cherished long after the event ends. Hiring a professional photographer can ensure high-quality snapshots of group activities and candid moments, but setting up a DIY photo booth can also add a fun element to your gathering. Provide props and a backdrop and let family members snap their pictures with cameras or smartphones. Additionally, creating a shared digital photo album through platforms like Google Photos or Dropbox can allow everyone to contribute their images and videos, creating a comprehensive and shared memory bank of the reunion. This digital collection can be a wonderful way to relive the joy of the gathering and keep the family feeling connected, even when apart.

In planning and executing a family reunion, the joy lies in the event and the anticipation of bringing loved ones together. Through careful planning, thoughtful activity selection, and capturing and sharing the memories created, you ensure that the reunion is not just a gathering but a milestone event that celebrates and strengthens familial bonds, leaving everyone involved with a sense of belonging and happiness. As you move forward with these plans, remember that the ultimate goal is to celebrate the unique tapestry of your family, making every moment count.

5.5 Neighborly Acts: Building Bonds in Your Community

Simple Gestures of Kindness

Small acts of kindness can weave strong connections between you and your neighbors in the fabric of daily life, transforming your neighborhood into a tightly knit community. Consider the simple joy that comes from sharing a batch of home-baked cookies with the family next door or helping a neighbor rake leaves in the fall. These gestures, small yet profound, can bridge gaps between neighbors, fostering a spirit of camaraderie and goodwill. For instance, if you enjoy gardening, sharing your garden's bounty offers not only the fruits of your labor but also an invitation to connect and engage in conversation. Similarly, offering to help with a neighbor's yard work can be particularly appreciated by those who might struggle with such tasks, such as elderly residents or busy parents. Through these actions, you demonstrate a sense of community spirit and open the door to mutual assistance and gratitude that enrich the lives of everyone involved.

Engaging in these acts of kindness requires little more than a willingness to step forward and a small investment of time or resources, yet the rewards are significant. Building relationships through these gestures fosters a supportive and friendly neighborhood environment where people look out for each other. This sense of belonging can be exceptionally comforting as you navigate the various stages of retirement, ensuring that you feel connected and valued within your community. Moreover, the ripple effects of your kindness often encourage others to act similarly, cultivating a culture of generosity and cooperation that can transform the entire neighborhood.

Organizing Block Parties or Potlucks

Organizing neighborhood events such as block parties or potlucks is a fantastic way to bring neighbors together in a relaxed and enjoyable setting. These gatherings can break down barriers and build friendships, strengthening community ties. To organize a successful block party, consult with your neighbors to choose a suitable date and time, ensuring maximum participation. You should obtain a permit from your local municipality, especially if you plan to block off a street. Once the logistics are set, distribute invitations clearly stating what each household should bring, such as dishes for a potluck, chairs, or games for children.

During the event, facilitate activities that encourage mingling and interaction among neighbors. Traditional street games like tug of war or sack races can be fun for all ages, or you could organize a bake-off or chili cook-off to add a competitive yet friendly element to the food offerings. Providing a communal space where neighbors can share food and laughter creates lasting memories. It strengthens the fabric of your community, making it a safer and more enjoyable place to live.

Creating a Neighborhood Association

Consider the benefits of forming or joining a neighborhood association for more structured community engagement. Such associations play a crucial role in addressing community issues collectively, from organizing neighborhood watch programs to planning local beautification projects. They provide a formal avenue for residents to voice concerns, propose solutions, and work together towards common goals, fostering a sense of empowerment and cohesion among members.

Starting a neighborhood association typically involves gathering a group of interested neighbors, electing a board to oversee activities, and setting up regular meetings to discuss issues and plan events. Regular communication through newsletters or social media can keep everyone informed and engaged. As an active member of a neighborhood association, you can contribute to making tangible improvements in your community by enhancing local parks, improving safety measures, or organizing community events. This involvement enriches your neighborhood and provides a sense of achievement and belonging.

Community Safety Initiatives

Taking a role in promoting safety in your community can significantly enhance the well-being of all residents. Initiatives such as neighborhood watch programs bring neighbors together to monitor each other's properties, reducing crime and increasing security. Organizing safety workshops with local police can also provide valuable information on crime prevention and safety tips, equipping residents with the knowledge to protect themselves and their homes.

Participating in these safety initiatives helps reduce crime and strengthens community bonds as neighbors come together with a common purpose. The increased communication and cooperation can lead to a more harmonious living environment where residents feel secure and connected. By taking an active role in these initiatives, you create a safer, more caring community where everyone can enjoy a higher quality of life, free from the worry of safety concerns.

5.6 Pet Adoption for Companionship: What to Consider

The decision to welcome a pet into your home during retirement can bring a new source of joy and companionship into your life. Pets offer affection and friendship, encourage a more active lifestyle, and provide a sense of purpose. Caring for a pet can significantly enrich your daily routine, offering unconditional love and the kind of loyalty that every human craves. Furthermore, caring for a pet can help structure your day, providing regular exercise and social interactions during walks or visits to the park. This can significantly boost both your physical and emotional well-being.

Choosing the right pet is critical when considering pet adoption and should align with your lifestyle and physical capabilities. For instance, a high-energy dog may require long walks and active play, which might be suitable if you enjoy outdoor activities and have good physical fitness. On the other hand, a cat or a smaller dog breed, which requires less space and exercise, is better suited if you live in an apartment or have mobility issues. It's also important to consider the pet's age. At the same time, puppies and kittens are adorable; they require much time, energy, and training. Older pets can be less demanding and may already be trained, making them potentially more suitable for a calmer retirement lifestyle.

Understanding the responsibilities involved in pet care is crucial before making a decision. Regular vet visits are necessary to maintain your pet's health, including vaccinations, dental care, and routine check-ups. You will also need to consider the daily responsibilities of feeding, grooming, and exercise, all of which require time and energy. Additionally, you should consider the financial aspect of pet ownership, including food, veterinary bills, grooming, and possibly pet insurance. Preparing for these responsibilities ensures you can provide your new companion a loving and stable home.

Finding a reputable pet adoption agency or animal shelter is the next step when you're ready to adopt. Organizations such as the ASPCA or local shelters typically have a process to help match the right pets with the right owners. These organizations can provide valuable information about the pet's history, health, and behavior, helping ensure that your new companion is a good fit for your home. Many shelters also offer post-adoption support and resources, which can be incredibly helpful as you integrate your new pet into your life.

Adopting a pet can be one of the most rewarding decisions you make during your retirement, providing companionship and a new avenue for love and care. As you consider the type of pet that would best suit your lifestyle, remember that this decision involves a commitment to care for and cherish a living being who can greatly enrich the quality of your life. With the proper preparation and consideration, pet ownership can add a fulfilling new chapter to your story, filled with joy and mutual affection.

Connecting to the Bigger Picture

In this chapter, we've explored various ways to enhance your social connections and build a supportive community network during retirement. From volunteering and joining senior centers to starting clubs and organizing family gatherings, each activity offers unique opportunities to engage with others and enrich your social life.

CHAPTER 6
TRAVEL AND ADVENTURE

Retirement travel is not just about visiting new places; it's a thrilling adventure that enriches your life and broadens your horizons. Each destination has a unique story to tell, every culture offers a fresh perspective, and every journey can create a treasured memory. Whether it's the charming streets of a European village, the bustling markets of Asia, or the tranquil beaches of the Caribbean, each place offers a distinct encounter and insight. This chapter is your guide to planning and enjoying travels that are not only fulfilling but also perfectly tailored to your needs and aspirations, sparking a sense of adventure and discovery in your retirement years.

6.1 Planning Your Bucket List Trip: Step-by-Step Guide

Identifying Dream Destinations

Start by envisioning the destinations you've always wanted to explore. What places come to mind when you think about your dream travel experiences? Is it the romantic landscapes of Tuscany, the historic ruins of Greece, or the majestic wildlife of Africa? Take a moment to list these destinations, and consider what draws you to them—is it their history, nature, culture, or cuisine? This exercise of identifying your dream destinations and understanding what attracts you to them is not just a fun activity, but a crucial step in setting clear travel goals. These goals will help you prioritize your destinations and plan your trips more effectively, ensuring that your travel choices align with your deepest interests and desires.

Budget Planning

Effective budget planning is essential to enjoy a stress-free trip that doesn't strain your finances. Start by determining how much you can spend on your travels. Consider all aspects of the trip, including transportation, accommodations, meals, entertainment, and shopping. Researching your destination can help you gauge the cost of living and travel expenses there. Tools like budget travel websites and cost comparison sites can offer insights into affordable travel options and daily expense estimates.

Additionally, setting up a dedicated savings plan for your trip can help you accumulate the necessary funds without impacting your regular financial obligations. Remember to explore travel insurance options, which can protect you against unexpected travel issues and health emergencies. A clear and detailed budget helps manage your expenses and ensures peace of mind throughout your journey.

Itinerary Planning

Creating a balanced itinerary with ample downtime is vital to enjoying your trip without feeling overwhelmed. Start by outlining the major attractions or activities you want to include, then spread them out over the days you'll be there, allowing for leisure time in between. This balance between sightseeing and relaxation is key to enjoying your trip to the fullest. Utilize travel planning tools and resources like travel blogs, guidebooks, and travel apps to find information on must-see sites and hidden gems. Booking flights, hotels, and activities in advance can save money and secure your spot, especially during peak travel seasons. When planning, consider your physical comfort and energy levels—plan heavier activities for mornings or early afternoons and lighter, more relaxing ones for later in the day.

Health and Mobility Considerations

Selecting the right destination is crucial for travelers with health or mobility issues. Look for places known for their accessibility and healthcare facilities. Before traveling, consult with your healthcare provider to ensure your health needs are taken care of; this might include securing medications, understanding how to manage your health condition while traveling, and knowing where the nearest hospital or medical facility is located at your destination. Research hotels and tourist attractions to confirm they meet your accessibility needs, such as elevator access, wheelchair ramps, and accessible transportation. These health and mobility considerations are not just precautions, but essential steps to ensure that your travel experience is comfortable, safe, and enjoyable, allowing you to explore with confidence and ease.

Travel is more than movement from one place to another; it's a pathway to new experiences and joyous discoveries that can enrich your retirement years immeasurably. Whether you're exploring ancient civilizations, indulging in exotic cuisines, or simply soaking in the scenic beauty of a peaceful landscape, every trip you take is a chapter added to your life story. With careful planning and a spirit of adventure, your travels can offer relaxation and exhilaration, crafting memories you'll treasure forever. Embrace each journey with an open heart and a curious mind, and let the world reveal its wonders to you one destination at a time.

6.2 Senior Travel Clubs: Joining Group Tours

Senior travel clubs offer a delightful blend of adventure, comfort, and social interaction, making them an ideal choice for those who want to explore the world with like-minded individuals. One of the key advantages of group travel is the structured, worry-free nature of the itineraries. These clubs handle all the logistical details—such as transportation, accommodations, and scheduling of activities—leaving you free to fully enjoy the experience. Moreover, traveling in a group setting provides a ready-made social network, allowing you to form new friendships and share memorable experiences with others who share your interests. Group discounts on travel services and activities are another significant perk, making this an economically attractive option as well.

Finding the right travel club that aligns with your travel style and interests is crucial for a fulfilling experience. Start by researching clubs that specialize in senior travel. Look for organizations with solid reputations and positive reviews from past travelers. Evaluating the types of trips they offer is essential to ensure they align with your preferences—whether you're interested in leisurely cruises, cultural tours, or nature excursions. Attending travel club meetings or informational sessions can also provide insights into the club's operations and offer a preview of their upcoming trips. This is also a great way to meet current members and ask questions about their experiences, which can help gauge whether the club's culture and pace match your travel desires.

Understanding and adapting to group dynamics is essential when traveling with senior clubs. Group travel often requires compromises on itinerary choices and dining options, which may involve adjusting to the group's overall pace. To integrate smoothly into the group, keep an open mind and be flexible with your preferences. Participating actively in group activities and discussions can help you connect with other members and enhance your overall experience. It's also helpful to establish clear communication with your tour leader and fellow travelers, especially regarding your personal needs or concerns. This cooperative approach ensures that everyone's experience is enjoyable and that the group functions well as a unit.

Senior travel clubs often offer a variety of tours that cater specifically to the interests and capabilities of older adults. Popular options include cultural tours that explore historic sites and local traditions, providing a deeper understanding of the destinations visited. These tours often include expert guides who provide insightful commentary and answer questions, enriching your knowledge and appreciation of the culture. Nature excursions are another favorite, offering opportunities to experience the natural beauty of scenic locations at a comfortable pace. River and ocean cruises are excellent choices for those who enjoy a more relaxed travel style. These trips allow you to unpack once and enjoy a variety of destinations and onboard activities, all while traveling in comfort. Each tour type is designed to offer safe, accessible, and engaging travel experiences, ensuring that you can explore the world in comfort and style.

As you consider joining a senior travel club, remember that this option provides a gateway to exploring new destinations, a wonderful avenue to meet new people, and a way to create lasting memories. With all travel details handled by experienced professionals, you can confidently embark on each trip, knowing that you're in good hands and free to enjoy every moment of your adventure.

6.3 Accessible Travel Destinations and Tips

When planning your travels, choosing destinations known for their accessibility can significantly enhance your experience, ensuring comfort and ease throughout your journey. Cities that are celebrated for their accessibility often feature well-designed public transportation systems, barrier-free attractions, and a general sensitivity towards travelers with mobility or health concerns. These destinations go beyond mere compliance with regulations; they are places where inclusivity is woven into the fabric of the community. For instance, cities like Vienna and Barcelona have invested heavily in making their public transport systems fully accessible, including low-floor trams and buses and elevators and ramps in their metro stations. Attractions in these cities are also thoughtfully designed to ensure that everyone can enjoy what they offer regardless of mobility. Before booking your trip, a thorough research phase is crucial. Start by visiting official tourism websites, which often provide detailed accessibility guides. Additionally, engaging with online forums such as TripAdvisor's Travel Forum or specific accessibility-focused platforms can offer insights from other travelers' experiences, which can be invaluable in planning your trip.

Securing accommodation and transportation that meet your needs is another critical aspect of travel planning. When booking accommodations, it's important to communicate directly with the hotel or rental property to confirm specific accessibility features. For instance, you might need to ensure there are no steps to enter the property, that there is a roll-in shower, or that door widths are adequate for a wheelchair. Similarly, when arranging transportation, whether for flying, taking trains, or renting vehicles, discuss your needs in detail with service providers. Many airlines and train companies offer the option to book assistance services in advance, including escorting you through the terminal, providing priority boarding, or ensuring that mobility aids are handled correctly. For car rentals, several companies specialize in vehicles modified for accessibility, offering features like hand controls or wheelchair lifts. Making these arrangements well in advance secures the services you need and gives you peace of mind.

Travel aids and resources are also vital for a comfortable journey. Various tools can make traveling more accessible, such as portable mobility devices, which are lightweight and easy to transport. These might include foldable wheelchairs, travel scooters, or walking aids designed to be conveniently stowed during a flight or in a vehicle. Knowing where to rent these aids at your destination can be a game-changer. Many major cities offer rental services for mobility devices, and some even deliver to your hotel. Additionally, apps like Wheelmap can help you locate accessible restaurants, cafes, and public facilities, significantly enhancing your travel experience. These tools empower you to maintain your independence and enjoy your travels with fewer limitations.

Understanding your rights as a traveler with disabilities is the final cornerstone of planning accessible travel. Various international and national laws protect these rights, ensuring that service providers in the travel industry accommodate travelers with disabilities. Familiarizing yourself with these rights can help you advocate for yourself when necessary. For example, in the United States, the Americans with Disabilities Act (ADA) provides comprehensive guidelines and protections for travelers. Similarly, the European Union has regulations in place that require airports and airlines to assist passengers with disabilities. If you ever feel your rights need to be respected, speaking up is essential. Contacting the service providers' customer service departments or contacting relevant regulatory bodies can often resolve issues. Knowing that you are backed by law adds an additional layer of security, allowing you to assert your needs and ensure that your travels are both possible and enjoyable.

Exploring the world should be accessible to everyone, and by choosing the right destinations, making detailed arrangements for accommodations and transport, utilizing helpful travel aids, and understanding your rights, you can experience the joys of travel comfortably and confidently. Each step taken to ensure accessibility benefits you and contributes to a broader movement towards more inclusive travel, encouraging destinations and service providers to improve their facilities and services for all travelers.

6.4 Cultural Immersion: Experiencing New Traditions and Customs

When venturing into a new country, immersing yourself in its cultural tapestry can transform a simple visit into a profound experience. A thoughtful preparation phase focused on understanding local customs and traditions is essential to truly engage with a new culture. This enriches your travel experience and fosters respect and appreciation between you and your hosts. Begin by exploring reliable resources such as cultural guidebooks, respected travel blogs, and even documentaries that focus on the cultural norms of the destination. Local tourism websites often provide visitors with invaluable cultural etiquette tips, such as appropriate dress codes in religious sites or customary greetings that show respect. Additionally, participating in cultural forums online can offer personal insights from other travelers and locals, giving you a deeper understanding of what to expect and how to conduct yourself sensitively.

Participating in local activities and festivals is a vibrant way to dive into the heart of any culture. These events offer a glimpse into the traditions and celebrations cherished by the local community. To find these opportunities, check the event calendars on local tourism websites or contact local cultural centers, which often have listings of upcoming events. Engaging with these activities allows you to experience the culture's most dynamic form—from traditional dances and music to local crafts and ceremonies. For instance, attending a traditional tea ceremony in Japan or a vibrant carnival in Brazil can provide enjoyment and a rich context to the cultural significance these traditions hold. When participating, it's important to approach each experience openly and respectfully, embracing the opportunity to learn and share in these cultural expressions.

Language plays a pivotal role in connecting with new cultures. Learning basic phrases in the local language not only eases daily interactions but also signals respect and effort on your part to engage with the community. Simple words like "Hello," "Please," "Thank you," and "Goodbye" can go a long way in fostering goodwill. Many language learning apps offer quick and accessible lessons on essential phrases that are useful for travelers. Spending a little time practicing these can make your interactions smoother and more enjoyable. Moreover, locals often appreciate any attempt to communicate in their language, which can lead to richer, more authentic experiences and interactions during your travels.

Culinary experiences offer a delicious gateway into a culture's traditions and values. Food reflects a community's history, environment, and beliefs, and participating in culinary activities can provide profound insights into the local way of life. Enrolling in cooking classes can give you a hands-on experience with traditional cooking methods and ingredients, often led by local chefs who share their culinary skills and stories and history behind the dishes. Additionally, guided market tours can introduce you to many local produce and spices and teach you how these are used in everyday cooking. These culinary adventures allow you to bring a piece of the culture back home, where you can recreate traditional dishes and share your experiences with friends and family, keeping the memories and flavors of your travels alive in your kitchen.

Exploring a new culture through its norms, festivities, language, and food does more than enhance your travel experience; it builds bridges of understanding and appreciation that enrich both the visitor and the host community. As you step into a new country with a spirit of curiosity and respect, you open yourself up to experiences that can transform the way you see the world. Through cultural immersion, travel becomes more than just a visit—it becomes a meaningful exchange that enriches your life and broadens your perspective.

6.5 Road Trips and Scenic Drives: Planning Short and Long Journeys

Planning Your Route

The freedom of the open road, with its endless horizons and spontaneous detours, beckons to the adventurous spirit in all of us. Planning your route for a road trip involves more than just selecting your start and end points; it's about crafting a journey that's as enjoyable as the destination itself. Start by mapping out the main route using reliable GPS technology or an updated road atlas. Consider the scenic value of different routes—sometimes, a longer path offers more breathtaking views and exciting locales, turning the drive into a highlight of your trip.

While charting your course, look for interesting stops—quaint towns, historical landmarks, or natural wonders—that can provide delightful breaks and enrich your travel experience. Apps like Roadtrippers or Google Maps can be invaluable here, helping you discover hidden gems often overlooked by traditional travel guides. Additionally, consider your comfort and energy levels; plan for regular rest stops to stretch, eat, or relax. These breaks keep you refreshed and ensure that you remain alert and enjoy the journey safely.

When planning longer journeys, think about overnight accommodations. Whether you prefer rustic campgrounds, cozy bed and breakfasts, or reputable hotels, booking in advance can save you the stress of finding last-minute lodgings. Websites like TripAdvisor or Airbnb offer user reviews and ratings, helping you find accommodations that meet your preferences for comfort and location. This careful planning ensures that every day of your road trip is balanced with driving and relaxation, making your travel experience both enjoyable and rejuvenating.

Vehicle Preparation

Before setting out on your road trip, ensuring your vehicle is in top working condition is paramount. This preparation is not just about comfort—it's crucial for your safety. Begin with a thorough vehicle check a few weeks before departure. The engine, brakes, tires, and batteries are key areas to focus on. Ensure the oil is changed, fluids are topped up, and the brakes are responsive. For tires, check the pressure and tread depth to ensure they are safe for extended driving, particularly in varied weather conditions.

If you are not conducting these checks yourself, a visit to a professional mechanic can provide peace of mind. Ask for a comprehensive inspection and address any issues they recommend fixing. It's also wise to check that your roadside assistance and car insurance are up to date to cover any unexpected situations. An emergency kit in your car, with items like a jumper cables, spare tire, a flashlight, and basic tools, can also prepare you for unforeseen mechanical issues. This preparation allows you to focus on enjoying your journey and be secure in knowing that your vehicle is as ready for the adventure as you are.

Packing Essentials

Packing for a road trip is an art form—it's about finding the perfect balance between preparedness and flexibility. Start with a checklist of essentials to ensure you don't forget anything vital. Your list should include navigation tools like GPS or maps, a first-aid kit, and enough snacks and water for the journey. Depending on your destination, you might also need specific gear like hiking boots, swimwear, or cold-weather clothing.

Consider the comfort of your vehicle's interior, especially if you'll spend several hours driving daily. Items like a lumbar support pillow or seat cushion can significantly affect your comfort levels. Also, pack a small cooler to keep perishable snacks fresh, and bring reusable water bottles that you can refill along the way to stay hydrated. Organizational tools such as backseat organizers or trunk dividers can help keep your car clutter-free, making it easier to find what you need when you need it. By packing smartly, you ensure that your road trip is enjoyable and harmonious.

Staying Energized and Engaged

Long stretches on the road can sometimes lead to fatigue, but there are many ways to stay energized and engaged. Audiobooks and podcasts are great companions for solo travelers, turning hours behind the wheel into entertainment or learning opportunities. Choose from a wide range of genres and topics to keep your mind stimulated and the journey interesting. For those who enjoy music, create a playlist of your favorite songs tailored to your travel destination to enhance the atmosphere of your trip.

Regular breaks are crucial, not just for physical comfort but also to rejuvenate your mind. Pull over at a rest stop or a scenic lookout every few hours to stretch your legs and breathe in some fresh air. If you're traveling with companions, consider fun road trip games that involve everyone, like "I Spy" or trivia questions about the places you're visiting. These activities help pass the time and create joyful memories of your shared journey. Keeping your body active and your mind engaged transforms every mile into a delightful part of your adventure, not just a route to your destination.

6.6 Safety Tips for Senior Travelers: Staying Secure on the Go

Traveling allows you to experience the joy of discovering new places and cultures. However, ensuring your safety and health during travels is paramount, especially for senior travelers facing unique challenges. Being prepared and aware can transform your travel experiences into enjoyable, worry-free adventures. Let's explore some essential safety practices, health precautions, and practical tips to keep you secure and healthy while you explore the world.

Personal Safety Practices

When traveling, the excitement of new environments can sometimes distract from personal safety. It's crucial to remain vigilant and cautious to protect yourself and your belongings. Keep your valuables like passports, money, and credit cards secured and close to your body in a money belt or a secure, zippered bag. Be especially mindful in crowded places like markets, tourist attractions, and public transport, where pickpockets are often active. Additionally, make an effort to blend in as much as possible. Tourists are often easy targets for scams, so dressing like a local and refraining from displaying expensive jewelry or cameras can help reduce unwanted attention.

Being aware of your surroundings is another crucial aspect of staying safe. When exploring new cities or areas, always have a basic idea of your route and destination. Avoid less populated and poorly lit areas, especially at night, and always have a plan for getting back to your hotel or accommodation. In case of emergency, familiarize yourself with the local emergency numbers and keep a list of these, along with the address and phone number of your country's embassy or consulate, accessible at all times.

Health Precautions

Staying healthy while traveling is just as important as staying safe. Before embarking on your travels, consult with your healthcare provider to discuss any necessary vaccinations or health precautions specific to your destination. This is particularly important for travel to regions where certain diseases, such as yellow fever or malaria, are prevalent. Ensure you have a sufficient supply of any regular medications you take and carry these in your carry-on luggage to avoid loss. It's also prudent to bring a small travel health kit with basic first aid supplies and medications for common travel-related ailments such as motion sickness, allergies, or minor cuts and bruises.

Knowing how to access medical care abroad is essential. Research hospitals or clinics near your destinations that offer services in English and accept your health insurance. If you have a pre-existing medical condition, carry a letter from your doctor that describes the condition and any prescriptions, including their generic names. If you're traveling to a country where English isn't widely spoken, having this information translated into the local language can be incredibly helpful.

Emergency Contacts and Information

A robust emergency plan can provide peace of mind when exploring far from home. Keep a list of emergency contacts, including family members, close friends, and your health care provider, and always ensure it's easily accessible. In addition, carry a list of your medications, allergies, and important health information. This information should be in a place that is easy to find, such as your wallet or with your travel documents, so it can be quickly accessed by medical personnel if you're unable to communicate. It's also wise to inform family or friends of your travel itinerary and check in on a regular basis. Hence, someone always knows where you are. Consider setting up a regular check-in schedule via phone call, text, or email, which can also reassure your loved ones back home.

Insurance and Documentation

Travel insurance is an essential tool for any traveler. Ensure that your policy covers medical emergencies, trip cancellations, and lost luggage, particularly if you're heading to a remote or volatile region. Read the fine print and confirm that your insurance provides sufficient coverage for your specific needs, including any adventure activities you plan to undertake. Keep copies of all your important documents—passport, insurance policy, emergency contacts, and health information—in a secure place separate from the originals. Digital copies stored securely online can also be handy in case of loss or theft. Traveling as a senior should be an enjoyable and enriching experience, free from undue stress about safety or health. By taking these precautions, you can safeguard your well-being and focus on the joys of discovering new destinations. With your safety and health secured, you're free to embrace the adventures that await, knowing you're well-prepared for whatever comes your way.

As we conclude this chapter on safety tips for senior travelers, we've covered essential practices and preparations to ensure your travels are both enjoyable and safe. Keeping these guidelines in mind, you can confidently embark on your adventures, ready to explore the world and its myriad cultures and landscapes.

CHAPTER 7
EMOTIONAL HEALTH AND PERSONAL GROWTH

I magine each day of your retirement not just as a series of hours to fill but as an opportunity to cultivate serenity and joy and to deepen your understanding of yourself and the world around you. This chapter invites you into the gentle practice of mindfulness and meditation. This journey promises to enhance your emotional resilience, reduce stress, and elevate your daily experiences to moments of profound clarity and peace.

7.1 Mindfulness and Meditation: Techniques for Peace and Clarity

Introduction to Mindfulness

Mindfulness is the art of being fully present and engaged with the here and now without distraction or judgment. At its core, mindfulness involves a calming plunge into the current moment, appreciating it in all its richness. The benefit of this practice is impactful for seniors. Mindfulness has been scientifically shown to decrease stress and anxiety, improve attention and memory, as well as emotional health. It can transform how you interact with the world, turning routine activities into moments of joy and deep connection.

Simple Meditation Practices

For those new to meditation, the prospect might seem intimidating. Still, the practices can be straightforward and easily integrated into daily life. One basic technique is focused breathing, where you pay attention to your breath, noticing the air moving in and out of your body. This practice can anchor you in the present moment and help clear the mind of clutter. Another effective technique is guided imagery, where you visualize a peaceful setting—maybe a quiet beach at sunset or a marvelous forest glade—and immerse yourself in sensory details to enhance relaxation and focus. These practices can be done anywhere, from a quiet room in your home to a bench in a bustling park, making them versatile tools for cultivating tranquility.

Incorporating Mindfulness into Daily Life

Integrating mindfulness into your daily life can enhance your awareness and appreciation of life's simple pleasures. Start with routine activities, such as eating a meal or taking a walk. Pay attention to your food's flavors, textures, and smells as you eat. When walking, notice the feel of the ground under your feet and the sounds around you. This intentional focus can turn ordinary experiences into rich, enjoyable moments, helping to cultivate a more mindful, gratifying lifestyle.

Resources for Deepening Practice

Numerous resources are available for those interested in deepening their mindfulness and meditation practices. Apps like Headspace and Calm offer guided meditations, mindfulness exercises, and educational content to help you build a consistent practice. Additionally, books such as "Wherever You Go, There You Are" by Jon Kabat-Zinn and "The Miracle of Mindfulness" by Thich Nhat Hanh provide insightful guidance and practical exercises. Local classes, often available at community centers or through wellness clinics, provide structured learning and the support of a group setting, which can be particularly motivating. These resources make it easier to explore mindfulness and meditation more deeply, enhancing your ability to maintain balance and peace in your retirement years.

Cultivating a Practice of Mindfulness

To encourage mindfulness practice, consider setting aside a few minutes each day for meditation. Start with just five minutes in the morning or evening, gradually increasing the time as you become more comfortable with the practice. Creating a designated space in your home for meditation—such as a quiet corner with a comfy chair or cushion—can also help establish a routine. Remember, the goal of mindfulness is not to empty your mind of thoughts but to observe them and let them pass, returning your focus to the chosen object of meditation. Over time, this practice can lead to greater emotional resilience and a deeper enjoyment of life's daily experiences.

By embracing mindfulness and meditation, you equip yourself with powerful tools to navigate the complexities of retirement with grace and poise. These practices offer a pathway to a more peaceful mind and a joyfully engaged life, enriching your days with clarity and calm. As you continue to explore these techniques, they will enhance your emotional health and enrich your relationships with others, bringing a greater depth of connection and understanding to your interactions.

7.2 The Power of Gratitude: Keeping a Daily Journal

Gratitude, a simple yet profound practice, can significantly alter your outlook on life, especially during retirement. Regularly acknowledging and appreciating the good in your life can enhance your mood, decrease stress, and cultivate a pervasive sense of well-being. Maintaining a gratitude journal, in which you regularly record moments and things you are thankful for, is a practical way to foster this mindset. Research in positive psychology consistently shows that individuals who focus on gratitude experience greater emotional well-being and resilience than those who do not. This practice helps shift focus from what may be lacking to the abundance in your life, promoting a positive emotional spectrum and reducing the frequency and intensity of negative feelings such as envy, resentment, and frustration.

Starting a gratitude journal is both simple and rewarding. Choose a journal that feels personal and pleasant to use—a beautifully bound book or a simple notepad, whatever resonates with your aesthetic preferences. The key is consistency, so aim to write in it daily, perhaps making it a relaxing ritual before bedtime or a reflective moment with your morning coffee. Begin by dating each entry, which can help you easily track your progress and reflect on past entries. Initially, write down three things you are grateful for each day. These can be as significant as family relationships or as simple as a delicious meal or a warm, sunny day. Writing these points down helps solidify them in your mind and makes the practice more tangible.

To enrich your journaling experience and stimulate your thoughts, consider using prompts that guide your reflections and deepen your insights. Some prompts might include: "What is something beautiful I saw today?" "Who is someone I'm grateful for and why?" or "What recent experience am I thankful for, and what did it teach me?" These questions encourage you to look beyond the surface and explore the more profound significance of your daily experiences. Over time, this practice not only boosts your mood and outlook but also enhances your attentiveness to the positive moments throughout your day, which you might otherwise overlook.

Sharing your gratitude can amplify its benefits, turning a personal practice into an opportunity to strengthen relationships and spread positivity. Consider discussing your gratitude journal entries with friends or family members, which can deepen your relationships and encourage others to reflect on their own sources of gratitude. This sharing can be particularly uplifting during gatherings where everyone shares something they are grateful for, fostering a collective appreciation and strengthening the bonds between everyone present. This communal practice multiplies the joy and builds a shared framework of gratitude and support, enriching your social interactions and emotional connections with those around you.

Incorporating gratitude into your daily life through journaling and sharing creates a powerful ripple effect that enhances your emotional landscape and enriches your interactions with others. As you continue this practice, you may discover a profound shift in how you perceive and engage with the world, finding joy and gratitude in places you might have previously overlooked. This shift can transform everyday experiences into sources of joy and meaning, making your retirement years richer and more fulfilling.

7.3 Navigating Life Transitions: Coping with Change

Retirement brings a mosaic of changes—some anticipated, others unexpected. You may find yourself adjusting to a fixed income, facing new health challenges, or dealing with the loss of loved ones. Each of these transitions requires not just practical adjustments but also emotional resilience. Recognizing and understanding these shifts as integral parts of your life's evolution can help you manage them gracefully and positively.

Adjusting to a fixed income can be one of the more tangible transitions. It often means re-evaluating your spending habits and lifestyle choices. Creating a detailed budget for your essential needs and leisure activities can provide a clear picture of your financial landscape. It's also helpful to explore new avenues for cost-saving, whether through senior discounts, budget-friendly travel options, or economical hobbies as previously discussed. This financial recalibration ensures that you live within your means and alleviates anxiety over money, allowing you to enjoy your retirement fully.

Health issues are common in aging, and new medical concerns can feel daunting. Proactively managing your health by attending regular medical check-ups, adhering to treatment plans, and maintaining a healthy lifestyle are critical steps. Equally important is the psychological adjustment to health challenges, which may involve modifying activities you used to perform. Adopting a mindset that focuses on what you can do rather than your limitations can significantly enhance your quality of life. Engaging in adapted physical activities, connecting with support groups, or learning new skills that accommodate your health needs can transform these challenges into opportunities for growth.

Losing a spouse or close friend is one of the most challenging transitions. Such losses can create profound grief that might seem insurmountable. During these times, leaning on a supportive network of friends, family, and community resources is crucial. Participating in grief counseling or support groups where you can share your feelings and hear others' experiences can be incredibly therapeutic. These settings provide solace and coping strategies to help you navigate your grief. Remember, mourning is a deeply personal process; allowing yourself to experience all emotions without judgment is part of healing.

Strategies for Managing Change

Embracing change, especially during retirement, requires deliberate strategies that foster adaptation and growth. Seeking support from peers, counselors, or family members can provide emotional comfort and practical advice as you navigate these changes. Expressing your concerns and experiences openly allows you to gain different perspectives. It reassures you that you are not alone in facing these challenges.

Setting new goals is another effective strategy for managing change. These goals provide a sense of direction and purpose, counteracting feelings of loss or confusion that might accompany major life transitions. Your goals can be as ambitious as starting a new venture or as simple as improving your garden. What matters is that they motivate you to look forward and take action, which is a powerful antidote to stagnation and despair.

Staying physically active is essential not only for your physical health but also for your emotional well-being. Regular exercise releases endorphins, natural mood lifters, which can help alleviate stress and anxiety. Walking, swimming, or yoga can be adapted to your fitness level. They can provide daily structure and social interaction. Moreover, a physical activity routine can bring a comforting predictability in times of change, providing a stable anchor in your daily life.

Building Resilience

Building resilience against the inevitable changes life throws your way involves cultivating a mindset that embraces challenges as opportunities for growth. This mindset, often called a 'growth mindset,' can dramatically influence how effectively you cope with transitions. It encourages adaptability, learning, and perseverance rather than a fixed or defeatist attitude. One way to develop this mindset is through reflective practices such as journaling, where you can explore your responses to changes and progress toward acceptance and adaptation.

Developing a solid social network is also crucial in building resilience. Relationships with friends, family, and community members provide emotional support, practical help, and a sense of belonging. These connections can be particularly empowering as you navigate through changes, offering a sounding board and a source of comfort. Community activities or volunteer work can expand your social network and strengthen your ties, providing a solid foundation that supports you through life's transitions.

Seeking Professional Help

Sometimes, the emotional weight of life's transitions may feel overwhelming, and it's important to recognize when professional help might be needed. Seeking assistance from counselors or therapists to help adults navigate retirement and aging issues can be incredibly beneficial. These professionals can offer coping strategies, therapeutic interventions, and ongoing support to help you effectively manage the complexities of change.

Support groups can also provide critical support, whether focused on grief, health issues, or life transitions. These groups offer a platform to share experiences and learn from others facing similar challenges, fostering a sense of community and mutual support. Many find these groups invaluable for finding strength and validation during difficult times.

Navigating life's transitions is undoubtedly challenging, but managing these changes effectively with the right strategies and support is possible. By seeking support, setting new goals, staying active, building resilience, and reaching out for professional help when needed, you can adapt to and thrive during the changes that come with retirement. Each step in managing these transitions helps you cope with immediate challenges and strengthens your capacity to handle future changes, enhancing your overall well-being and quality of life.

7.4 Rediscovering Passions: Turning Interests into Projects

Rediscovering and nurturing hidden passions can dramatically enrich your retirement, transforming routine days into periods of exploration and personal achievement. Often, during the hustle of career or family life, many of your inherent interests or hobbies may have been shelved. Retirement opens a unique window of opportunity to revisit these sidelined passions or discover new ones. Begin this exciting phase by reflecting on activities that once brought you joy or subjects you've always been curious about but never had the time to explore. Did you once love painting or playing a musical instrument? Have you always been fascinated by history or astronomy? List these interests without judgment, allowing yourself to acknowledge all areas that spark your curiosity.

Once you have identified what excites you, the next step is planning how to engage with these interests meaningfully. For instance, if you find joy in gardening, consider starting a small herb garden or volunteering at a community garden. If writing is your passion, consider starting a blog or writing short stories. This phase is about setting the foundation for what could evolve into your passion project. Gather information about what you'll need to begin: materials, courses, or joining a club or group. This exploration stage is crucial as it lays down the practical steps to transform your interest into a tangible project.

Setting achievable goals for your passion projects is essential to ensure they remain enjoyable and stress-free. Begin with small, manageable objectives that encourage regular engagement and gradual progress. For example, if you're interested in photography, set a goal to learn one new photography skill each week, or if you're gardening, aim to plant a new type of flower each month. These goals should challenge you slightly but remain within reach to maintain motivation and a sense of accomplishment. Remember, these projects aim to enrich your life, not to add stress, so adjusting your goals to ensure they remain enjoyable is important.

Celebrating milestones in your passion projects is crucial for sustaining motivation and recognizing progress. Whether it's finishing a painting, performing a new music piece, or successfully growing your first batch of vegetables, take the time to celebrate these achievements. You might share your accomplishments with friends and family or treat yourself to something special in recognizing your hard work. Documenting these milestones can also be rewarding; keeping a photo journal or writing about your project's progress in a diary can be an excellent way to reflect on your journey and appreciate how far you've come. These celebrations remind you of your capabilities and reinforce the joy and satisfaction of pursuing your passions.

As you delve into these rediscovered or newly found interests, allow yourself to fully enjoy learning and growing. Each step forward in your passion project builds your skills and enriches your understanding of yourself and what you can achieve. This ongoing engagement with your interests can significantly enhance your sense of self and overall satisfaction with life, making your retirement years truly golden.

7.5 Giving Back: Mentorship and Sharing Your Knowledge

Giving back, particularly through mentorship, offers an opportunity for personal growth and community engagement. As you navigate the later stages of life, you may find yourself in possession of invaluable wisdom and experience—a treasure trove of knowledge that can significantly impact the lives of others. Exploring avenues for mentorship can be as fulfilling for you as it is beneficial for those you guide. Local schools, community centers, and online platforms provide diverse opportunities to connect with individuals or groups who can benefit from your insights. For example, volunteering as a reading mentor at a local school can help children develop a love for books while enhancing their reading skills. Community centers often seek experienced individuals to lead workshops or talks on various topics, from gardening to personal finance. Online, virtual mentorship has grown, allowing you to connect with mentees worldwide, sharing your professional experience or life skills through video calls and webinars.

The mutual benefits of engaging in mentorship are substantial. As a mentor, you gain a renewed sense of purpose. This role allows you to contribute positively to someone else's life, validating your life experiences and knowledge as valuable assets that can guide others. This exchange often leads to a deep sense of satisfaction and accomplishment. Furthermore, the process of mentoring can stimulate your own intellectual and emotional growth. Engaging with mentees frequently challenges you to think critically, communicate effectively, and be empathetic—skills that are as enriching as they are essential for personal development. For the mentee, the benefits are just as impactful. They receive guidance, encouragement, and support that can make a significant difference in their personal and professional growth, fostering their development and helping them navigate their challenges more effectively.

When considering becoming a mentor, it's essential to approach this role with intentionality and mindfulness. Effective mentorship is rooted in the ability to listen actively. This means fully concentrating on what your mentee is saying without planning your response while they speak. It involves engaging with their thoughts and feelings, asking clarifying questions, and offering thoughtful and constructive feedback. Another critical aspect of successful mentorship is setting clear boundaries. These help define the relationship from the outset, clarifying what each party can expect regarding time commitments, confidentiality, and the mentorship goals. Clear boundaries ensure that the relationship remains professional and focused, which benefits both mentor and mentee.

Lastly, consider your unique skills and experiences as you contemplate stepping into a mentorship role. Every individual has unique experiences that have shaped their lives and perspectives. Reflect on these experiences and see how they can benefit others. Your unique attributes are valuable, whether it's your professional expertise, life lessons learned from overcoming challenges, or skills developed through hobbies or interests. By sharing your knowledge, you aid others in their personal and professional development and leave a lasting legacy that transcends your immediate environment, potentially impacting future generations.

In essence, mentorship is a reciprocal relationship that offers deep fulfillment and growth for both mentor and mentee. It's a testament to the power of sharing knowledge and the profound connections that can result from it, enriching lives and communities in meaningful ways. As you embark on this path, you embrace a role that highlights the best of what you can offer, reinforcing your value and potential to effect positive change. This engagement enriches your life and plants seeds for the future, cultivating a legacy of knowledge and kindness that endures.

7.6 Exploring Spirituality: Finding Meaning and Comfort

Spirituality, a deeply personal journey, can manifest in myriad forms, from structured religious practices to more personal, meditative activities. Each person's spiritual path is unique, shaped by individual beliefs and experiences. Spirituality often deepens during retirement, which can bring introspection and the pursuit of a deeper understanding of life's profound questions. Whether through participation in organized religion, private meditation, or simply observing nature, spiritual practices provide a framework to explore one's beliefs and find comfort in the continuity of life.

Broadening the Concept of Spirituality

Spirituality extends beyond traditional religious practices; it encompasses any activity that helps you connect to something greater than yourself, fostering a sense of peace and purpose. For many, this could mean involvement in organized religious institutions where rituals and community gatherings provide a sense of belonging and structure. For others, spirituality might be more reflective, involving meditation, yoga, or leisure time in nature. Exploring different spiritual practices can enrich your understanding of what resonates with your personal beliefs and values, helping you to cultivate a practice that brings inner peace and clarity. This exploration might lead you to read spiritual texts, engage in discussions about philosophy and ethics, or participate in community service, each offering different pathways to spiritual fulfillment.

Spiritual Practices for Daily Life

Integrating spirituality into your daily routine can enhance your connectedness and overall well-being. Simple practices like prayer or meditation in the morning can set a positive tone for the day, grounding you in your spiritual beliefs. Similarly, taking walks in nature can be a form of moving meditation, offering opportunities to reflect on the beauty of the natural world and its cycles, which can be exceptionally comforting. Another practice could be the daily reading spiritual or philosophical texts, which can offer insights and guidance. These practices provide comfort and help cultivate a routine prioritizing your spiritual health, giving you tools to cope with daily stresses and uncertainties.

Connecting with Spiritual Communities

Finding and joining a community that shares your spiritual values can significantly enhance your spiritual journey. These communities offer support, understanding, and the joy of exploring spiritual life with others. Local churches, temples, meditation groups, or online forums can be valuable for connecting with like-minded individuals. These groups often organize events, workshops, and group discussions, which can provide deeper insights into spiritual practices and beliefs. Participating in community services or group rituals can also be profoundly fulfilling, enhancing your connection to others and spiritual beliefs.

The Role of Spirituality in Coping with Aging

As you navigate the later stages of life, spirituality can provide a sense of peace, purpose, and continuity. It can offer solace in times of loss or change and provide a perspective that celebrates the cycle of life with all its endings and beginnings. Spiritual beliefs can give reassurances of life's continuity in some form, which can be exceptionally comforting.

Furthermore, spiritual practices can help maintain an attitude of gratitude and acceptance, enhancing resilience against the challenges that aging can bring. This aspect of spirituality is about coping with the challenges and appreciating life's journey, with all its intricacies and experiences.

As this chapter closes, we reflect on how spirituality can enrich your retirement years. From providing deep personal solace and a framework for understanding life's greater purpose to offer practical daily practices that enhance emotional and mental health, spirituality can be a profound source of comfort and joy.

CHAPTER 8
CREATIVE AND CULTURAL PURSUITS

I magine turning your moments into timeless treasures, capturing the fleeting beauty of everyday life through the lens of a camera. More than just a hobby, photography is a gateway to preserving memories, discovering minute details of the world around you, and expressing your unique perspective. It's an art form that invites you to slow down, observe, and connect deeply with your surroundings—an enriching pursuit that can add value and joy to your golden years.

8.1 Photography: Capturing Life's Moments

Photography as a Hobby

Photography stands as a powerful medium that bridges generations and illustrates personal narratives without the need for words. As a hobby, photography offers more than just the joy of capturing images; it encourages mindfulness and an active engagement with your environment. Focusing on framing a shot can be a meditative practice, requiring you to present in the moment, keenly aware of details that might otherwise go unnoticed. This attentive observation encourages a deeper appreciation for the beauty of the everyday world, from the intricate patterns of a flower to the vibrant scenes of a street market. Moreover, as you grow more comfortable with a camera, you'll see the world through a different lens—spotting photo opportunities in ordinary settings, understanding the interplay of light and shadow, and capturing the unique stories around you.

Tips for Taking Great Photos

Several practical tips for seniors embracing photography can make the process more enjoyable and the results more rewarding. A tripod can help stabilize the camera, especially in low-light conditions, reducing the blur caused by hand movements. This is particularly useful when taking long-exposure photos where even slight shakes could impact the sharpness of the image. Learning to use the camera's settings, such as aperture, shutter speed, and ISO, allows you greater creative control over how the photos turn out. Aperture affects the depth of field, shutter speed influences the depiction of motion, and ISO determines the camera's sensitivity to light. Exploring these settings can transform your photographs from ordinary to extraordinary.

Sharing and Preserving Memories

Once captured, photographs can become a part of your legacy, shared and cherished by family and friends. Digital platforms like social media and cloud storage services such as Google Photos or iCloud make it easy to share these captured moments instantly with loved ones, no matter where they are. For those who prefer physical copies, options abound for printing photos in various formats—from traditional prints to put in an album to larger framed pieces for home decor. Creating photo books can also be an excellent way to chronicle life's adventures, themed around trips, events, or even everyday moments, providing a tangible collection of memories to browse through and pass down through generations.

Photography, in its essence, is about connection—to the moments, the world, and each other. It offers a fulfilling way to engage with the world through the lens and the heart. As you explore this captivating hobby, let each shutter click capture a scene and celebrate your unique worldview, preserving the precious whispers of life that might otherwise fade away.

8.2 Dance Classes: From Ballroom to Ballet at Home

Dancing, a delightful blend of art and exercise, offers a unique combination of physical and mental stimulation that can be particularly beneficial in your golden years. Whether you've always had a rhythm in your step or just discovered your dancing shoes, exploring various dance styles can bring a fresh zest to your life. With its elegance and partner coordination, ballroom dancing offers a beautiful opportunity for social interaction and physical closeness, which can be pretty fulfilling. Line dancing, with its repetitive patterns and group dynamics, is excellent for those who prefer a more casual and less physically demanding style. Ballet, though more challenging, strengthens the core, improves posture, and enhances flexibility. Each style holds distinct benefits; ballroom dancing enhances coordination, line dancing can boost cardiovascular health, and ballet improves flexibility and balance.

Creating a dedicated space at home for dancing can transform part of your living environment into a vibrant dance floor. Start with ensuring the flooring is suitable—hardwood floors are ideal as they provide a smooth, flat surface that minimizes the risk of falls and facilitates more effortless movement. If changing your flooring isn't an option, consider a large, non-slip rug or a portable dance mat that can provide a safe area to dance. The space should be free of obstacles, and furniture should be rearranged to create ample room for movement. Proper lighting and a good sound system can also enhance the experience, making your dance practice safe and enjoyable. Mirrors along one wall are a great addition as they help monitor and correct your posture and technique as you dance.

The digital age makes it easier than ever to learn dancing from the comfort of your home. Numerous online platforms and DVDs are available that cater specifically to beginners and seniors. These resources often offer step-by-step tutorials you can follow at your own pace, breaking down complex dance moves into manageable steps. Look for programs designed with seniors in mind, focusing on gentle movements and flexibility exercises crucial for your safety and comfort. Websites like LearntoDance.com offer a variety of dance lessons online, and many community centers provide virtual classes that you can join live, allowing you to interact with an instructor and receive feedback in real-time.

The health benefits of dancing are as joyful as the activity itself. Regular dance practice can significantly improve your balance and flexibility, reducing the risk of falls, a common concern as we age. The rhythmic movements of dance help build strength and endurance. Cardiovascular health also sees a boost from the aerobic nature of most dance routines, helping to keep your heart healthy and strong. Beyond the physical, dancing stimulates the mind, requiring you to remember steps and sequences, which can enhance cognitive function and memory. The emotional uplift from moving to music is another profound benefit, often releasing endorphins that can reduce stress and depression. Dancing can be a holistic practice, enriching your physical and emotional health as well as mental well-being.

As you glide, tap, or leap, remember that each movement is a step toward a healthier, more joyful you. Dancing tunes your body and harmonizes your soul, making it a perfect symphony of health and happiness. So, whether you waltz in your living room or tango through an online class, embrace the rhythm of life with each step. Your dance floor awaits right in your own home, ready for you to make your move.

8.3 Visiting Theaters and Museums: A Guide for Seniors

Exploring the rich tapestry of culture through theaters and museums offers more than just entertainment and education; it is a way to connect with the vibrant currents of human expression and history. As you plan these enriching outings, consider the myriad of factors that can transform a simple visit into a seamless and enriching experience. Begin by identifying the best times to visit—weekday mornings often provide a quieter environment, allowing you to absorb exhibits or performances without the hustle of larger crowds. Many theaters and museums offer special discounts for seniors, so it's beneficial to inquire about reduced rates or even free entry days, making these cultural excursions both affordable and enjoyable.

Accessibility is another crucial aspect, ensuring your visit is comfortable and hassle-free. Most modern institutions have ramps, elevators, and hearing loop systems. Still, it's always prudent to call ahead and confirm these details. Some venues also offer special tours or performances tailored for seniors, featuring enhanced audio for easier listening or guided tours that take a slower pace, allowing for a more leisurely and accessible experience.

Engaging actively with the arts during your visits can significantly enhance the richness of the experience. Participate in guided tours, often led by knowledgeable individuals who can provide deeper insights into the exhibits or performances. These tours can offer fascinating historical contexts and hidden stories behind the artworks or productions, enriching your understanding and appreciation. Many theaters and museums also host special senior days, where events are specifically designed to cater to older adults, encouraging social interaction and shared learning experiences. Joining discussion groups post-visit can also be incredibly rewarding; these forums provide a space to reflect on and discuss your impressions and interpretations with fellow art lovers, enhancing your cognitive engagement and social interaction.

Discovering local cultural gems requires a bit of curiosity and exploration. Beyond the well-trodden paths of major museums and theaters, many communities boast smaller, less-known venues that offer unique and intimate cultural experiences. Local art galleries, community theaters, and historical museums often feature exhibits and performances that reflect the area's specific cultural nuances and histories. These smaller venues can also provide more personal interaction with the art and artists, often at a fraction of the cost of larger institutions. Engage with local tourism offices or community boards, or even explore online community forums and social media groups dedicated to arts and culture in your area. Here, you can uncover hidden cultural treasures in your backyard, offering fresh and exciting opportunities for cultural engagement.

Extending the cultural experience beyond the initial visit can keep the inspiration and learning alive. After visiting an exhibit or watching a performance, consider diving deeper into the themes or histories presented. Reading books or watching documentaries on similar topics can expand your understanding and appreciation of what you've experienced. Many museums offer catalogs or companion books that delve into their collections or special exhibits in more detail. For theatergoers, reading the play beforehand or exploring reviews and analyses can provide greater insight into the nuances of the performance. Engaging in these extended learning experiences enhances your cultural literacy. It enriches your overall enjoyment and appreciation of the arts, making each visit a step closer to deeper understanding and connection.

8.4 Crafting: Projects for Every Season

Crafting, a delightful exploration of creativity and manual skill, offers joy and fulfillment that resonates deeply during retirement. As the seasons change, they bring unique inspirations and opportunities for crafting projects that beautify your home and enrich your spirit. Imagine crafting bright floral arrangements in spring, vibrant beach-themed decorations in summer, or cozy knitted scarves and hats as winter approaches. Each season holds its charm and challenges, making crafting an ever-evolving source of pleasure and creativity.

In spring, the world awakens with bursts of color and life, making it the perfect time for gardening projects or floral crafts. You might start by planting a functional and therapeutic herb garden, providing fresh ingredients for your kitchen and a lush green space in your home. Crafting with flowers, such as creating your own wreaths or assembling beautiful bouquets, can also be a delightful way to bring spring indoors. As summer arrives, consider projects like decorating beach hats or creating custom tote bags, perfect for visits to the beach or picnics in the park. These projects stir creativity and cater to practical uses, enhancing your summer activities.

When autumn rolls in, the palette shifts to warm oranges, browns, and reds, inspiring projects like making autumn leaf candle holders or crafting Halloween or Thanksgiving decorations. These crafts can add a festive spirit to your home and are excellent activities to share with grandchildren, creating memories and beautiful objects. Winter crafts include knitting, crocheting, or making holiday cards and decorations. These activities not only fill the longer evenings but also help keep you warm and engaged, producing practical and gift-worthy items.

Finding suitable materials for these projects is crucial, especially when looking for options that are both accessible and senior-friendly. Both online and locally, craft stores offer a wide range of supplies. Still, choosing those that are easy to handle and pose minimal frustration is essential. Look for ergonomically designed tools that are easier on the hands and materials that are simple enough to work with. Many stores also offer pre-assembled crafting kits, which can be very handy. These kits usually come with step-by-step instructions and all the necessary materials, simplifying the process and ensuring you have everything you need to complete a project successfully.

Joining or forming a community crafting group can significantly enhance your crafting experience. Not only does it provide a social outlet, an essential aspect of maintaining mental and emotional health, but it also allows for the sharing of ideas, techniques, and resources. Local crafting groups might be advertised at community centers and libraries or in local shops. If there isn't one nearby, consider starting your own. This can be as simple as inviting a few friends to bring their projects to your living room once a week or reaching out through community boards or online platforms to find like-minded individuals. Organizing such a group helps you connect with others and provides a regular appointment to look forward to, which can be a great motivator.

The benefits of engaging in crafting are profound. Beyond the apparent joy of creating something with your hands, crafting can be a form of meditation, allowing you to focus intensely on a task and reduce stress. The tactile nature of handling materials and making deliberate, thoughtful movements can be incredibly soothing, offering a respite from the hustle and bustle of everyday life. Moreover, the sense of accomplishment that comes from completing a project can boost your self-esteem and provide a tangible reminder of your creativity and skill. Whether a handcrafted gift for a loved one or a decorative item for your home, each completed project adds more joy to your life.

With its endless possibilities, crafting offers a fulfilling way to celebrate the changing seasons, connect with others, and express your creativity. As you weave, paint, knit, or sculpt, you are not just creating art—you are crafting a rich, colorful tapestry of life in retirement. No matter how small, each project is a testament to your creativity and a beacon of joy in your everyday life.

8.5 Culinary Exploration: Trying Global Cuisines at Home

Embarking on a culinary journey in the comfort of your own kitchen can be an amazing experience, offering a taste of adventure and the warmth of home-cooked meals. Exploring world cuisines provides a delightful avenue to experience diverse cultures through the universal language of food. From the robust flavors of Italian pasta dishes to the zesty and aromatic delights of Thai cuisine, each recipe brings its own story and an opportunity to broaden your culinary horizons. Preparing these dishes at home diversifies your diet. It enhances your cooking skills, making each meal exciting and rewarding.

Begin with simple, well-loved recipes from various cultures that don't require rare ingredients or complex cooking techniques. For instance, an Italian pasta carbonara or a classic Thai green curry can bring the essence of these countries into your dining room. These dishes typically require ingredients readily available at local supermarkets or can be easily substituted without compromising authentic flavors. Preparing these meals can also become a cherished ritual, turning an ordinary evening into a special occasion infused with the joy of exploration and the satisfaction of a delicious meal.

Cooking techniques specific to international cuisines can significantly elevate your culinary skills. For instance, mastering the art of perfect 'al dente' pasta or balancing the four fundamental Thai flavors—sour, sweet, salty, and spicy—can transform your cooking. Start by learning how to properly use spices, the heartbeat of many ethnic cuisines. Toasting spices before grinding them or adding them to your dish can release oils and aromas that deepen flavors dramatically. Basic knife skills, such as how to julienne carrots or finely chop herbs, speed up your prep work and ensure ingredients cook evenly, blending their flavors harmoniously.

Themed cooking nights can be an excellent way to share this culinary adventure with friends or family. Imagine an evening where each person brings a dish from a different country, creating a buffet that spans continents. Not only does this allow for a tasting tour around the world, but it also sparks conversations about food traditions and personal travel experiences. These gatherings can be informal and fun, with everyone contributing something to the table, from a homemade dish to a story about their chosen cuisine. It's a beautiful way to build connections and create memories centered around the joy of eating and sharing.

Enhance your culinary exploration by watching cooking shows and online videos that focus on international cuisines. These programs often provide more than just recipes; they delve into the culture and history behind the dishes, giving you a deeper appreciation for the food you're preparing. Chefs and culinary experts can also introduce you to cooking techniques and ingredient choices that are rooted in tradition, helping you understand the why behind the way foods are prepared in different parts of the world. This blend of entertainment and education is enjoyable. It enriches your cooking experience, providing you with knowledge that goes beyond the recipe.

As you continue to explore and experiment with global cuisines, each dish you create is more than just a meal; it's a passport to a new culture, a story on a plate, and an invitation to a broader world. Whether you're stirring a pot of fragrant curry or kneading dough for fresh pasta, you're not just cooking—you're embarking on exploring the rich tapestry of global flavors, all from the comfort of your kitchen. So, go ahead, pick a country whose cuisine excites you, and let the adventure begin—one recipe at a time.

8.6 Film and Literature: Hosting a Themed Movie or Book Night

Engaging in the arts of film and literature enriches your mind. It offers a beautiful opportunity to connect with friends and family through themed movie or book nights. These gatherings can transform an ordinary evening into a vibrant exploration of storytelling and character, where each film or book serves as a springboard for deeper discussion and connection. A thoughtful approach to selecting themes, organizing the gathering, and facilitating discussion is vital to ensure these events are as enjoyable and enriching as possible.

When choosing a theme for your movie or book night, consider genres and subjects that resonate with your interests and those of your guests. Classic film noir, with its intricate plots and moral ambiguity, can offer a lot of material for discussion. Alternatively, contemporary memoirs provide a personal glimpse into different lives and challenges, which can prompt reflective conversations. Themes can also be light-hearted; for example, choosing films or books that focus on travel adventures can be delightful, providing escapism and the joy of exploring new places from the comfort of your living room. The chosen theme should be broad enough to include various works yet specific enough to provide a cohesive thread for the evening.

Organizing a successful movie or book night involves more than selecting the proper film or book; it's about creating a comfortable environment where guests can relax and engage. Set up a viewing area where everyone can see the screen comfortably without crowding, perhaps rearranging furniture to ensure ample seating. Soft cushions and adjustable lighting can enhance the ambiance, making the space cozy and welcoming. For book discussions, ensure enough light for reading excerpts or notes and that seating allows for easy conversation. Providing themed snacks can also add fun and immersion to the event—think pastries for a French film night or iced tea and biscuits for a Southern novel discussion.

Facilitating engaging discussions after the movie or book can deepen the appreciation of the themes and characters explored. Prepare a few open-ended questions to prompt thought and conversation among your guests. These questions might examine the characters' motivations, the setting's relevance, or how the themes relate to contemporary issues or personal experiences. Encouraging guests to share their thoughts and feelings can lead to diverse interpretations and a richer understanding of the material. This makes the discussion more interactive and ensures that everyone feels included and valued in the conversation.

Incorporating technology can streamline access to a wide range of films and literature, making it easy to find and enjoy content relevant to your chosen theme. Streaming services offer an extensive library of movies and television shows that can be accessed at the click of a button, providing a convenient way to watch a chosen film together. E-readers and digital library services can be equally helpful in accessing books, especially out-of-print titles or new releases that may need to be readily available in physical form. Demonstrating how to use these technologies before the event can help ensure that all guests are comfortable and able to access the content, regardless of whether they are tech-savvy.

Hosting a themed movie or book night is a delightful way to explore the arts while enjoying the company of friends and family. You can ensure these evenings are memorable and meaningful by carefully selecting themes, creating a comfortable environment, facilitating enriching discussions, and utilizing technology. As each story unfolds, so does the opportunity for deeper understanding and connection, enriching your social interactions and enhancing your appreciation of film and literature.

As we close this chapter on creative and cultural pursuits, we reflect on the diverse ways you can engage with arts and crafts, enrich your culinary experiences, and delve into the worlds of cinema and literature, all from the comfort of your home. These activities are not just hobbies; they are gateways to learning, sharing, and exploring, continuing to enrich your life and bring joy in your retirement years.

CONCLUSION

As we draw near the conclusion of our shared journey, let us take a moment to reflect on the rich tapestry of possibilities that will unfold when retirement comes. We have explored various themes, from embracing technology to enriching our lives with budget-friendly activities, maintaining robust physical and mental health, engaging in continuous learning, and fostering deep social connections. Together, we have navigated the pathways of travel and adventure, delved into the importance of emotional health, and celebrated the joy of personal growth.

Retirement marks not the end of a career but the beginning of an exhilarating chapter brimming with opportunities to live with purpose and joy. This book has been crafted to equip you with the knowledge and tools to redefine your golden years as a period of vibrant exploration and meaningful engagement. Each page and chapter was designed to inspire you to fill your days with activities that bring pleasure and a profound sense of fulfillment.

The advice shared in these pages resonates with the importance of staying active and connected. Whether through physical activities that keep your body healthy or through social engagements that enrich your spirit, staying involved and interconnected forms the cornerstone of a joyful retirement. We also discussed how creativity and cultural appreciation can significantly enhance one's quality of life. Retirement can be the most enriching phase of your life by exploring new interests, learning new skills, and engaging with the world around you. Your willingness to embrace new experiences and expand your horizons will enrich your days and provide a continuous source of happiness and satisfaction.

I encourage you to take that first step on the pathway to and exciting and fulfilling retirement. Choose one activity or goal from this book to pursue immediately. Whether joining a local walking club, starting a digital photography project, or planning a long-dreamed road trip, take the initiative. Be open to new experiences and embrace this incredible journey enthusiastically and courageously.

It's important to acknowledge that physical, emotional, or social challenges may arise during retirement. However, armed with the right mindset and the strategies outlined in this book, you are well-prepared to overcome these hurdles. Remember, you are not alone on this journey. Each chapter has been designed to guide you and inspire and motivate you to navigate these challenges successfully.

I invite you to share your stories and retirement experiences with others. Engage with a community of fellow retirees, whether online or in person, to exchange tips, celebrate successes, and offer encouragement. Your stories are powerful and can inspire others just as they inspire me.

Thank you for allowing me to be a part of your retirement journey. It is my sincerest hope that this book serves as a valuable guide and a steadfast companion as you explore the many opportunities that await in your golden years.

Together, let's continue to discover the joy and satisfaction that this new chapter of life holds. Here's to your adventure-filled, enriching, and vibrant retirement!

REFERENCES

1. My Assured Home Nursing. (n.d.). 7 new tech gadgets for seniors to make life easier. Retrieved from https://myassuredhomenursing.com/blog/tech-gadgets-for-the-elderly-to-make-life-easier/
2. ConnectSafely. (n.d.). The senior's guide to online safety. Retrieved from https://connectsafely.org/seniors-guide-to-online-safety/
3. Ormsby Living. (n.d.). Best online learning platforms for older adults. Retrieved from https://www.ormsbyliving.org/about/news-blog/best-online-learning-platforms-for-older-adults/
4. Spring Hills. (n.d.). 10 immersive virtual reality experiences for seniors. Retrieved from https://www.springhills.com/resources/virtual-reality-for-seniors
5. LiveAbout. (n.d.). 10 free entertainment activities for seniors. Retrieved from https://www.liveabout.com/free-entertainment-activities-for-seniors-2969299
6. Rosterfy. (n.d.). The ultimate guide on how to start a volunteer program. Retrieved from https://www.rosterfy.com/blog/the-ultimate-guide-on-how-to-start-a-volunteer-program-in-9-steps
7. National Institute on Aging. (n.d.). Participating in activities you enjoy as you age. Retrieved from https://www.nia.nih.gov/health/healthy-aging/participating-activities-you-enjoy-you-age
8. HGTV. (n.d.). 70 DIY decor projects to craft this weekend. Retrieved from https://www.hgtv.com/design/make-and-celebrate/handmade/diy-decor-projects-to-craft-this-weekend-pictures
9. National Center for Biotechnology Information. (n.d.). Yoga for healthy aging: Science or hype? Retrieved from https://www.ncbi.nlm.nih.gov/pmc/articles/PMC8341166/
10. Spring Hills. (n.d.). 7 essential benefits of water aerobics for seniors. Retrieved from https://www.springhills.com/resources/water-aerobics-for-seniors
11. Age Safe America. (n.d.). Starting a walking club for older adults. Retrieved from https://agesafeamerica.com/starting-a-walking-club-for-older-adults/
12. National Center for Biotechnology Information. (n.d.). Tai Chi exercise for

mental and physical well-being. Retrieved from https://www.ncbi.nlm.nih.gov/pmc/articles/PMC9957102/
13. Senior Lifestyle. (n.d.). 10 best brain games for seniors & older adults. Retrieved from https://www.seniorlifestyle.com/resources/blog/best-brain-games-for-seniors/
14. Not Just Bingo. (n.d.). Guide for starting a book club for seniors. Retrieved from https://notjustbingo.com/articles-and-resources/quick-tips-for-activity-directors/assisted-living-book-club-for-senior-residents/
15. The Bristal. (n.d.). The best apps and tools for seniors to learn a new language. Retrieved from https://blog.thebristal.com/the-best-apps-and-tools-for-seniors-to-learn-a-new-language
16. Medium. (n.d.). Online art classes for older adults ease social isolation. Retrieved from https://medium.com/@sonyaphoto7/online-art-classes-for-older-adults-ease-social-isolation-during-pandemic-1fdc6a45cc05
17. AmeriCorps. (n.d.). Volunteering helps keep seniors healthy, new study suggests. Retrieved from https://americorps.gov/newsroom/press-releases/2019/volunteering-helps-keep-seniors-healthy-new-study-suggests
18. Kampgrounds of America. (n.d.). How to plan a family reunion. Retrieved from https://koa.com/blog/family-reunion-planning-guide/
19. Wag!. (n.d.). 3 heartwarming senior pet adoption stories. Retrieved from https://wagwalking.com/daily/3-heartwarming-senior-pet-adoption-stories
20. Lane, L. (2023, June 30). Best (and worst) destinations for senior travel according to new data. Forbes. Retrieved from https://www.forbes.com/sites/lealane/2023/06/30/best-and-worst-destinations-for-senior-travel-according-to-new-data/
21. AARP. (n.d.). 14 best senior travel groups that offer all kinds of adventures! Retrieved from https://community.aarp.org/t5/Destinations/%EF%B8%8F-14-Best-Senior-Travel-Groups-That-Offer-All-Kinds-of/m-p/2501720
22. National Council on Aging. (n.d.). Mobility-friendly travel guide. Retrieved from https://www.ncoa.org/adviser/medical-alert-systems/mobility-friendly-travel-guide/
23. I'm Thinking of Retiring. (n.d.). Cultural immersion experiences for older adults: A better way to travel. Retrieved from https://imthinkingofretiring.com/cultural-immersion-experiences-for-older-adults-a-better-way-to-travel/
24. National Center for Biotechnology Information. (n.d.). Mindfulness-based interventions for older adults. Retrieved from https://www.ncbi.nlm.nih.gov/pmc/articles/PMC4868399/

25. Greater Good in Action. (n.d.). Gratitude journal. Retrieved from https://ggia.berkeley.edu/practice/gratitude_journal
26. HelpGuide. (n.d.). Adjusting to retirement: Handling depression and stress. Retrieved from https://www.helpguide.org/articles/aging-issues/adjusting-to-retirement.htm
27. Legacy Senior Living. (n.d.). How senior mentors benefit from helping others. Retrieved from https://legacysl.net/senior-mentors-benefit-helping-others/
28. Samarth Community. (n.d.). The benefits of photography for seniors. Retrieved from https://samarth.community/lifestyle/benefits-of-photography-for-seniors/
29. SilverSneakers. (n.d.). Dance exercise classes for seniors. Retrieved from https://www.silversneakers.com/blog/video/dance-exercise-classes-for-seniors-dancing-classes/
30. Smithsonian National Museum of Natural History. (n.d.). Accessibility information. Retrieved from https://naturalhistory.si.edu/visit/accessibility
31. Taste of Home. (n.d.). 95 international recipes to make when you're craving global cuisine. Retrieved from https://www.tasteofhome.com/collection/travel-around-the-world-in-80-meals/

AUTHOR BIOGRAPHY

Neal M. Kenwick is a dedicated professional and family man living in the Northeastern United States with his wife, two kids, and their beloved dog.

Neal's home is full of activity and love. He and his wife create a warm, supportive environment for their children. The family enjoys spending time together, whether exploring nature, attending sports games, or relaxing at home.

Family is very important to Neal. He spends time with his parents and in-laws, who inspired his book and keeps them close in his and his children's lives. This close family bond reflects Neal's values of love and togetherness.

Printed in Great Britain
by Amazon